Grade 7-8
Summer Activity Playground

12 weeks of Summer Activities:

- → Math
- → ELA
- → Science
- → Reading
- → Social Studies

BRAIN HUNTER

Brain Hunter Prep is a division of ArgoPrep dedicated to providing high-quality workbooks for K-8th grade students. We have been awarded multiple awards for our curriculum, books and/or online program. Here are a few of our awards!

Our goal is to make your life easier, so let us know how we can help you by e-mailing us at: info@argoprep.com.

ALL RIGHTS RESERVED
Copyright © 2020 by Brain Hunter Prep

ISBN: 9781951048389
Published by Brain Hunter Prep.

All rights reserved, no part of this book may be reproduced or distributed in any form or by any means without the written permission of Argo Brothers, Inc. All the materials within are the exclusive property of Argo Brothers, Inc.

Aknowlegments:
Icons made by Freepik, Creaticca Creative Agency, Pixel perfect, Pixel Buddha, Smashicons, Twitter, Good Ware, Smalllikeart, Nikita Golubev, monkik, DinosoftLabs, Icon Pond from www.flaticon.com

- ArgoPrep is a recipient of the prestigious **Mom's Choice Award**.
- ArgoPrep also received the 2019 **Seal of Approval** from Homeschool.com for our award-winning workbooks.
- ArgoPrep was awarded the 2019 **National Parenting Products Award, Gold Medal Parent's Choice Award** and a **Brain Child Award**

Want an amazing offer from ArgoPrep?

7 DAY ACCESS to our online premium content at **www.argoprep.com**

Online premium content includes practice quizzes and drills with video explanations and an automatic grading system.

Chat with us live at **www.argoprep.com** for this exclusive offer.

Summer Activity Playground Series

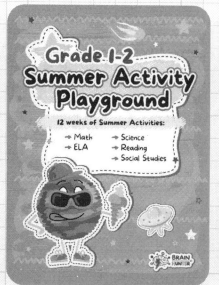
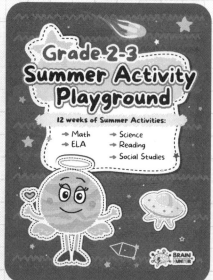
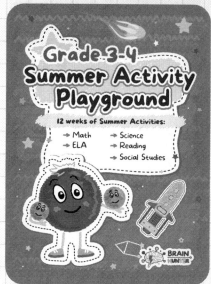
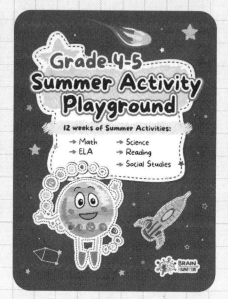
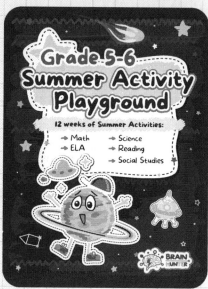

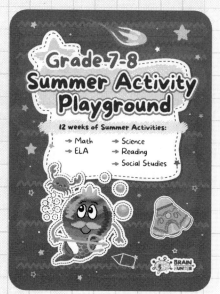

How to use this book?

Welcome to **Summer Activity Playground by Brain Hunter Prep!**

This workbook is specifically designed to prepare students over the summer to get ready for **Grade 8**. Our workbook is divided into twelve weeks so students can complete the entire workbook over the summer.

Our workbooks have been carefully designed and crafted by licensed teachers to give students an incredible learning experience. Students will be able to practice mathematics, english activities, science experiments, social studies, and fitness activities. Give your child the education they deserve!

Summer list to read

We strongly encourage students to read several books throughout the summer. Below you will find a recommended summer reading list that we have compiled for students entering into Grade 8. You can see this list at: www.argoprep.com/**summerlist**

Author : J. D. Salinger
Title : Catcher in the Rye

Author: Michelle Obama
Title: Becoming

Author: Douglas Adams
Title: The Hitchhiker's Guide to the Galaxy

Author: Isaac Asimov
Title: Foundation

Author: Joan Bauer
Title : Hope Was Here

Author: Robert Cormier
Title: The Chocolate War

Author: Charles Dickens
Title : A Christmas Carol

Author : Alexandre Dumas
Title : The Three Musketeers

Author : Russell Freeman
Title : We Will Not Be Silent

Author : Anita Lobel
Title: No Pretty Pictures

OTHER BOOKS BY ARGOPREP

Here are some other test prep workbooks by ArgoPrep you may be interested in. All of our workbooks come equipped with detailed video explanations to make your learning experience a breeze! Visit us at **www.argoprep.com**

COMMON CORE MATH SERIES

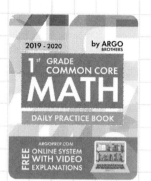 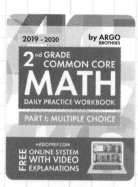 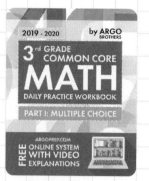 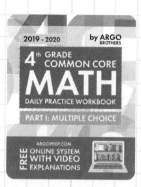

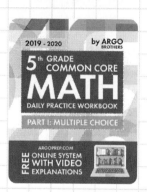 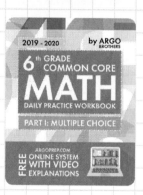 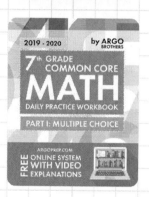 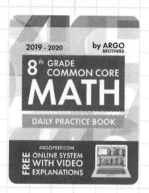

COMMON CORE ELA SERIES

INTRODUCING MATH!

Introducing Math! by ArgoPrep is an award-winning series created by certified teachers to provide students with high-quality practice problems. Our workbooks include topic overviews with instruction, practice questions, answer explanations along with digital access to video explanations. Practice in confidence - with ArgoPrep!

YOGA MINDFULNESS FOR KIDS

HIGHER LEVEL EXAMS

WORKBOOKS INCLUDED

Comprehensive K-8 Math & ELA Program

www.argoprep.com/k8

Math & ELA success begins here

Real Results, Close Learning Gaps, Boost Confidence

30,000+ Practice Questions

500+ Video Lectures

15,000+ of Video Explanations

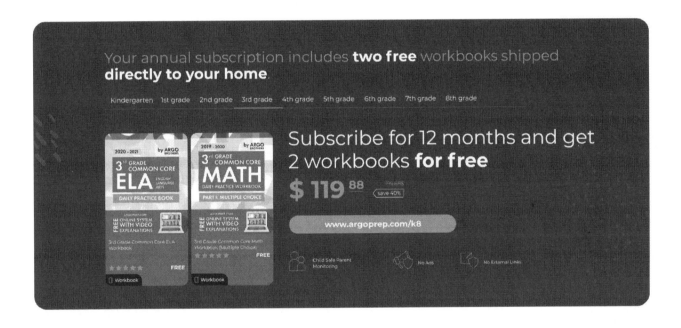

Printable
Worksheets, Games and more

Common Core
Next Generation Learning Standards & State Aligned

Grade 7-8
WEEK 1

Let's get started with:

- ✹ ratios
- ✹ compare/contrast structures
- ✹ the scientific method
- ✹ verbals and more!

Week 1 Math
Topic 1 Ratios

1. Tom bakes $\frac{1}{2}$ a batch of cookies in $\frac{3}{4}$ hour. At this rate, what fraction of a batch of cookies can Tom bake in 1 hour?

2. Helen folds $\frac{1}{8}$ of the towels in $\frac{2}{11}$ hour. At this rate, how many of the towels will she fold in 1 hour?

3. Jayden walks $\frac{4}{5}$ mile in $\frac{1}{4}$ hour. At this rate, how far will he walk in 1 hour?

4. Tina files $\frac{2}{7}$ of her papers in $\frac{3}{4}$ hour. At this rate, how much will she file in 1 hour?

5. Izzy swims $\frac{3}{7}$ of her laps in the pool in $\frac{4}{9}$ hour. At this rate, how many of her laps will she swim in 1 hour?

6. Jana plants $\frac{3}{8}$ of the flowers in the garden in $\frac{5}{11}$ hour. At this rate, how many of the flowers will she plant in 1 hour?

Week 1 Math
Topic 2 Constant of Proportionality (Unit Rate)

1. What is the constant of proportionality in the equation $y = 6x$?

2. What is the constant of proportionality in the equation $y = \frac{1}{3}x$?

3. What is the constant of proportionality between y and x?

x	3	6	9
y	1	2	3

4. What is the constant of proportionality between y and x?

x	1	2.5	4
y	4	10	16

5. Use the graph to determine the constant of proportionality, y:x

   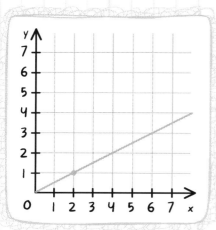

6. Use the graph to determine the constant of proportionality, y:x

   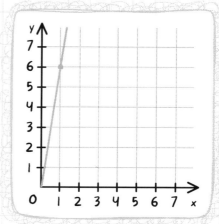

Week 1 Reading
Topic 1 — Compare and Contrast Structures

Key Vocabulary

- Milieu Structure - focuses on the world
- Idea Structure - focuses on finding something through a character's journey
- Character Structure - focuses on a character's growth, transformation, or downfall.
- Event Structure - seeks to fix a problem

Read these fictional stories. Then, answer the questions about structure that follow.

Passage One

Excerpt from Chapter 1 "Peter Breaks Through"
from *The Adventures of Peter Pan* by J.M. Barrie

Public Domain Material

Mrs. Darling, the mother of Wendy, John, and Michael, loved to have everything just so in her house, and she would tidy up the children's rooms, as well as their minds. You see, it is a nightly custom of every good mother after her children are asleep to rummage in their minds and put all of their thoughts straight for the next morning. This was essential to creativity and growth. It was quite like tidying up drawers and closets. Every evening, Mrs. Darling would tidy up all of her children's minds. She noticed that their minds were filled with colorful images of lagoons, flying flamingos, wigwams, and a land in which no one ever grew up. However, Mrs. Darling found one word and image that she could not understand, and that was "Peter". She knew of no one named Peter and wondered who he might be.

Week 1 Reading
Topic 1 Compare and Contrast Structures

Passage Two

Excerpt from Chapter 1 "Rachel Lynde is Surprised" in *Anne of Green Gables* by Lucy Maud Montgomery

Public Domain Material

One afternoon in early June, Mrs. Lynde was at her cherished location, which was her dining room window where she could see who goes in and out of Avonlea. "What in the world?" said Mrs. Lynde. She was aghast when she witnessed Matthew Cuthbert. She thought he should be in the fields like her husband, not on the road at half-past three. He was wearing a white-collared shirt and his best suit. Matthew so rarely went from his home; it must be something pressing and unusual, for he is the shyest man alive. He doesn't generally go to town this time of year and he never visits anyone. If he'd run out of turnip seed he would not be dressed up. And he was not driving swift enough for it to be an emergency. "I'm clean puzzled," said Mrs. Lynde, "and I won't know a minute's peace of mind or conscience until I know what has taken Matthew Cuthbert out of Avonlea today."

1. What is the structure of passage one? Explain.

2. How does the structure help readers understand this fictional story?

3. What is the structure of passage two? Explain.

4. How does the structure help readers understand this fictional story?

5. How do these two structures compare to each other? Explain.

6. How do these two structures differ? Explain.

 FITNESS PLANET → Let's get some fitness in! Go to page 167 to try some fitness activities.

Week 1 Science
Topic 1 The Scientific Method

There are different steps in the scientific method. The steps are listed below. Explain what each step entails.

Steps in the Scientific Method:

1. Identify the Question - ....
2. Develop the Hypothesis - ....
3. Test the Hypothesis - ....
4. Analyze the Data - ....
5. Draw Conclusions - ....
6. Communicate the Findings - ....

Read the paragraph below that explains someone going through the steps in the scientific method. When you recognize a step, write the number by the line.

A botanist realized that hydrangeas were different colors, and she couldn't figure out the rhyme or reason to why one hydrangea was blue, one pink, and another, purple. She planted a tray of hydrangeas and all nineteen in the tray were blue; however, the last tray on the right was purple. How in the world did that happen? She then tried it again when she went home in her garden that afternoon. After they grew, she realized that on one side of the garden, the hydrangeas were blue, in the middle they were purple, and on the other side they were pink. The botanist decided to test the soil in the garden and in the tray. She realized that there was a difference in the acidity (or pH) of the soil from one side of the tray/garden to the other. This made the botanist think that maybe the pH of soil could affect the color of this particular flower. The botanist decided to fill twelve trays with soil. Four of the trays had a pH of 4.5, the next four had a pH of 7, and the last four had a pH of 6.3. After they grew, the botanist smiled. In the first tray, the hydrangeas were blue, in the middle tray they were pink, and in the last tray they were purple. The botanist realized that the pH of the soil affected the colors of the hydrangea. She shared her findings with other botanists she knew and published an article of her findings in a magazine.

Week 1   Science
Topic 2   Identifying Terms

What are experimental and control groups?

Write the definition next to the term.

1. Experimental Group - ....

2. Control Group - ....

Read the passage below. Identify which is the control group and which is the experimental group.

Tara and Leo were making paper boats and racing them in a pool with the hose. They wondered if using construction paper would make the boat go faster. Tara folded her boat with regular lined paper, while Leo folded his paper in thick red construction paper.

Identify the groups.

3. Lined notebook paper boat - ....

4. Construction paper boat - ....

What are independent and dependant variables?

Write the definition next to the term.

5. Independent Variables - ....

6. Dependent Variables - ....

17

Week 1 — Math
Topic 3: Recognizing Proportional Relationships

1. Does the following table show a proportional relationship between x and y?

x	$\frac{1}{3}$	$\frac{2}{3}$	1
y	2	4	6

2. Does the following table show a proportional relationship between x and y?

x	5	10	15
y	0.5	1.5	2.5

3. Fill in the missing part of the table to make a proportional relationship between x and y.

x	?	18	36
y	1	3	6

4. Thad earns $26 for working 2 hours, $39 for working 3 hours and $52 for working 4 hours. Are Thad's earnings proportional to the number of hours he works?

5. At the beginning of summer, Phoebe has 50 math questions to complete. She will complete 2 of them every day. Is the number of questions Phoebe has left proportional to the number of days that pass?

6. Henry joins a movie club where his first 5 movies are free and then each movie is $10 afterwards. Is the amount of money Henry spends on movies proportional to the number of movies he owns?

Week 1 — Math
Topic 4: Comparing and Interpreting Constants of Proportionality

1. Which relationship shows a greater constant of proportionality between y and x?

A.
x	5	10	15
y	3	6	9

B.
x	$\frac{1}{2}$	1	$1\frac{1}{2}$
y	2	4	6

2. Mark took a road trip and wrote the equation $y = 55x$ to represent his distance, y, and number of hours driven, y. What does 55 mean in this situation?

3. Which graph shows a greater constant of proportionality between y and x?

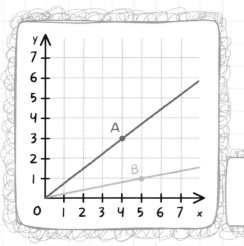

4. Rachel spent $6 on 4 avocados at the grocery store. The equation $y = 1.5x$ represents this situation where x is the number of avocados and y is the price. What does 1.5 mean in this situation?

5. The equation $m = 15c$ shows the number of lawns, c, mowed by Isla and the amount of money she earned, m. The equation $d = 18g$ shows the number of lawns, g, moved by Grace and the amount of money she earned, d. Who earned more per lawn?

FITNESS PLANET → Let's get some fitness in! Go to page 167 to try some fitness activities.

Week 1 Language Review
Topic 2 Verbals

Key Vocabulary

* Infinitives - contains the word "to" and a verb; can be used as a noun, an adjective, or an adverb
   * **EXAMPLE** - My horse wants **to trot** around the arena before the competition begins.

* Gerunds - ends in -ing; used as a noun
   * **EXAMPLE** - Walking is an easy and affordable form of exercise.

* Participles - ends in -ing or -ed; verb that is used as an adjective
   * **EXAMPLE** - I was the laughing stock of my class when I spilled milk all over myself.

Read the sentences below. On the line, identify the underlined verb. Write an I for an infinitive, a G for a gerund, or a P for a participle.

1. Currently, I am teaching my pet turtle <u>to roll</u> over on command. ......

2. <u>Eating</u> is my favorite activity during Superbowl parties. ......

3. My neighbors saved the pets from the <u>abandoned</u> building in the middle of winter. ......

4. My goals for the future are <u>to be</u> a pediatrician in an impoverished country. ......

5. Aaron's favorite winter hobby is downhill snow <u>skiing</u>. ......

6. My aunt was on <u>bended</u> knee in prayer when I came into the church. ......

7. My teacher uses spying as a strategy for catching sneaky behavior in class. ......

8. My <u>sewing</u> machine broke last Tuesday, so I have to sew my skirt by hand. ......

Week 1 Reading
Topic 3 Context Clues and Vocabulary

When reading, you will come across many difficult vocabulary words. In doing so, it is important to use context clues to figure out what a difficult and unusual word means.

Read the sentences below. Then, using context clues, identify the definition of the bolded word. When finished, check the bolded words in a dictionary to see if you are correct.

1. For Halloween, Erica's **ostentatious** costume choice had the whole student body looking in her direction.

   Definition - ....

2. Ryan and Angelica **battled** each other on the difficult journey to be class president.

   Definition - ....

3. Arnold was removed from class and was issued a detention in **conjecture** of being involved in plagiarism.

   Definition - ....

4. Violet's **callous** teacher did not allow her to turn in her homework late, even though she missed class to attend her grandfather's funeral.

   Definition - ....

5. The prisoner was given **immunity** for his involvement in the crimes as a result of giving vital information to the FBI agents.

   Definition - ....

6. The **aristocrat** from England traveled to New York by private jet and was picked up at the airport in a white stretched limo.

   Definition - ....

Week 1   Math
Topic 5   Discount and Markup Problems

1. A jacket was originally $49 but is now on sale for 20% off. What is the new price?

2. An appliance store buys a refrigerator at a wholesale price of $650. If the markup rate at this store is 40%, what is the markup for the sofa?

3. All items in a bookstore are 10% off. Julia has a coupon for another 15% on top of any other discounts. She finds a book that costs $22 originally. How much will it cost after both discounts?

4. Garrett had been wanting to buy a new video game system that costs $200. When it went on sale for 30% off, he had enough money to buy it. How much did the system cost after the discount?

5. A clothing store has a markup rate of 60%. The new jeans that just arrived cost $13 wholesale. What is the retail price after the markup?

6. A car dealership has a markup rate of 3%. The wholesale price of a new SUV is $28,000. What is the markup for this SUV?

FITNESS PLANET → Let's get some fitness in! Go to page 167 to try some fitness activities.

Week 1 Social Studies
Topic 1 The Bill of Rights

The Bill of Rights includes the first ten amendments in the Constitution.

The ten amendments are listed below. Explain each one and write down what would not be allowed according to that amendment.

1st Amendment
* Freedom from religion, speech, and the press

....

....

2nd Amendment
* The right to bear arms

....

....

3rd Amendment
* Does not allow for soldiers to house in private residents

....

....

4th Amendment
* Freedom from searches and seizures

....

....

5th Amendment
* Right to due process and self-incrimination

....

....

6th Amendment
* Right to a speedy trial

....

....

7th Amendment
* Right to trial by a jury of your peers

....

....

8th Amendment
* Freedom from cruel and unusual punishments

....

....

9th Amendment
* Rights of the people

....

....

10th Amendment
* Reserve of power to the states

....

....

Grade 7-8
WEEK 2

Now get ready to learn about:

* proportional relationships
* character development
* experimental protocol
* active/passive voice

and more!

Week 2 Math
Topic 1 Test for Equivalent Ratios

1. The ratio 5:12 is equivalent to 20 : ☐ ?

2. The ratio 18:4 is equivalent to ☐ :6?

3. True or false:
   The ratio 7 to 8 is equivalent to 21 to 25.

4. True or false:
   The ratio 14 : 1 is equivalent to 21 : 1.5.

5. Jen used 24 beads to make a 12-inch long necklace. Sydney wants to make a shorter necklace with the same ratio of beads to string. She uses 20 beads. How long should her string be?

6. When John makes chocolate chip cookie dough, he adds 12 ounces of chocolate chips for every 16 ounces of dough. When his brother Benji makes chocolate chip cookie dough, he adds 10 ounces of chocolate chips for every 14 ounces of dough. Whose chocolate chip cookies contain a higher ratio of chocolate chips to dough?

Week 2 Math
Topic 2 Proportional Relationships as Equations

1. For art class, the teacher tells the class to mix 2 parts red and 3 parts blue to make just the right shade of purple paint. Write an equation that relates r, the amount of red paint and b, the amount of blue paint to make this shade of purple.

2. Quentin harvests apples at a constant rate. He needs 15 minutes to harvest a total of 20 apples. Write an equation that describes the relationship between t, the time, and a, the total number of apples harvested.

3. The table below shows the cost to purchase different numbers of equally priced movie tickets. Write an equation that describes the relationship between t, the number of tickets, and c, the total cost of tickets.

Number of tickets	Cost
7	$66.50
13	$123.50
18	$171

4. The table shows a proportional relationship between c and d. Write an equation that describes the relationship between c and d.

c	d
22	33
31	46.5
40	60

5. The equation $d = 93t$ represents the distance (in miles), d, a bullet train travels in t hours. What is the constant of proportionality and what does it represent?

Week 2 Reading
Topic 1 Character Development in Nonfiction

Read the passage below. Then, answer the questions that follow.

A gifted and ingenious girl named Jaime, who resides in Boston, Massachusetts, has created her very own makeshift business at the budding age of eleven. Jaime sells lemonade and other lemon-themed delicacies at her makeshift lemonade stand that travels throughout the city. This lemonade stand is not traditional, as Jaime's lemonade is very different and unique. She does not just utilize lemons and sugar in her recipe, but she also includes a secret ingredient. Jaime spices up her lemonade by adding flavors and colored dyes. Her most popular flavor is the unicorn surprise.

When Jaime was six, she petitioned her mother to help her run a lemonade stand. She had this grandiose idea after witnessing other children her own age have one on her favorite Disney show growing up. Her mother wanted to boost her daughter's business ambitions, but she had a full time job, as well as a part-time job at an afterschool program in the evenings. Jaime's mother communicated with the administrator's at Jaime's school. There was a bake sale planned before an upcoming Christmas program to raise money for a local homeless shelter. Jaime's mother received permission for Jaime to start her lemonade stand at the bake sale.

With this newfound opportunity, Jaime immediately started concocting different flavors of lemonade as she didn't want to serve plain lemonade only. Since she knew she was starting her business at a bake sale, she also thought that she should serve bake sale items. Jaime went to work in the kitchen and made original lemon treats for her customers to enjoy. She made lemon sprinkle cookies, sugar lemon brownies, lemon cake pops, lemon cheesecake, and old fashioned lemon drop cookies.

Jaime's school's bake sale was a big hit, especially Jaime's lemonade stand. Before the Christmas program even started, Jaime was sold out of lemonade and all of her lemon flavored treats. After this initial showing, many individuals wanted Jaime to sell her lemonade and lemon flavored treats at different events and parties. Jaime's business was known throughout their town and it became very popular. Through her endeavors, Jaime has learned how to make a list of what items she needs, how to budget the cost of those items, how much time it will take to make everything, and how to brainstorm and taste new recipes.

  Let's get some fitness in! Go to page 167 to try some fitness activities.

Week 2 Reading

Topic 1 Character Development in Nonfiction

1. Describe Jaime's personality? Cite textual evidence.
   ....

2. What do others think and feel about Jaime? Cite textual evidence.
   ....

3. What are some implicit inferences you have made about Jaime? Cite textual evidence.
   ....

4. What positive skills does Jaime possess? Cite textual evidence.
   ....

5. Predicting, what do you think Jaime's future goals are?
   ....

Week 2 Science
Topic 1 Experimental Protocol

An experimental protocol includes is basically the steps you will complete in order to conduct an experiment. This also includes the materials that are needed for the experiment and the steps you will need to complete.

Below is an experiment protocol for diffusion. Follow the steps and then answer the questions below.

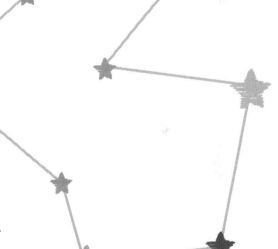

The materials you will need are:

* 2 clear glasses that are the same size
* Hot water
* Cold water
* Food dye
* Timers (2)

The steps that you will need to follow are:

* Pour hot water to the middle of one clear glass.
* Pour cold water to the middle of the other clear glass.
* Drip two drops of food coloring into both glasses.
* Start your two timers to see how long the food coloring spreads throughout each glass.
* When finished, write down the time it took for each glass and write it below.

* Hot glass - ....
  ....

* Cold glass - ....
  ....

29

Week 2 Science
Topic 1 Experimental Protocol

1. What is an experimental protocol? ....

2. What is diffusion? ....

3. What happened to the dye in both glasses? ....

4. What was different regarding the dye in both glasses? What did you notice? ....

5. What did you learn from this experiment? ....

Week 2 Math
Topic 3 Constant of Proportionality from Graphs

1. Use the graph to find the constant of proportionality, $\frac{y}{x}$.

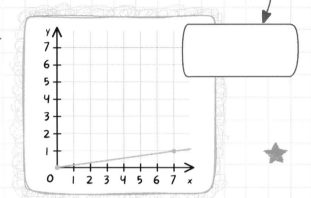

2. Use the graph to find the constant of proportionality, $\frac{y}{x}$.

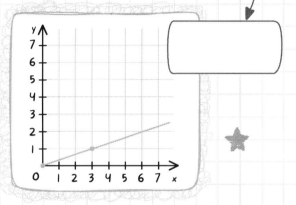

3. Use the graph to find the constant of proportionality, $\frac{y}{x}$.

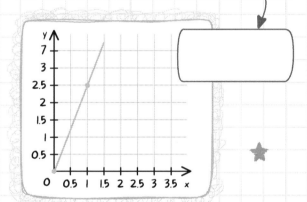

4. Use the graph to find the constant of proportionality, $\frac{y}{x}$.

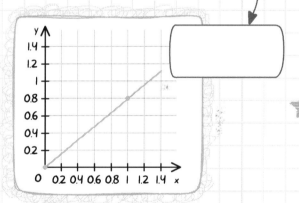

5. Use the graph to write an equation that describes the relationship between x and y.

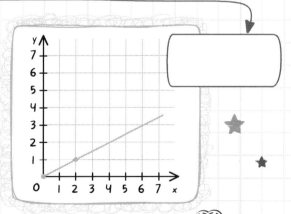

FITNESS PLANET → Let's get some fitness in! Go to page 167 to try some fitness activities.

31

Week 2 Math
Topic 4 Graphs of Proportional Relationships

1. The following graph shows the hours worked and wages earned of an employee. Find the employee's hourly wage.

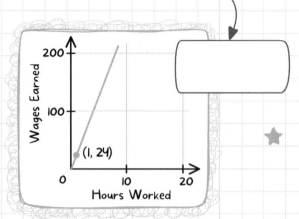

2. The following graph shows a proportional relationship between x and y. Find the constant of proportionality, $\frac{y}{x}$.

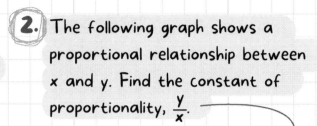
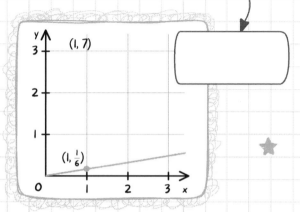

3. The following graph shows a proportional relationship between x and y. Find the constant of proportionality, $\frac{y}{x}$.

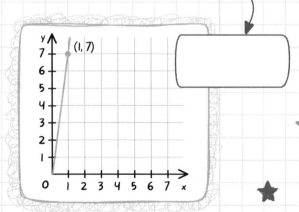

4. What is the constant of proportionality between y and x in the graph?

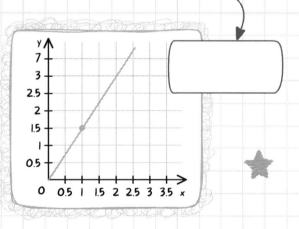

5. Which line has a constant of proportionality between y and x of 4?

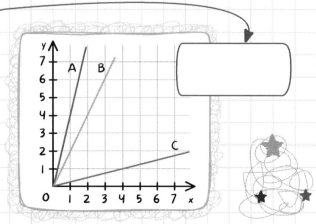

Week 2 Language
Topic 2 Active and Passive Voice

What is active and passive voice?

* Active and passive voice both contain action verbs.
* Active and passive voice differs in the subject of the sentence. Active voices is often used in academic writing.
* In active voice, the subject performs the action
    * **EXAMPLE** - I ate many burritos.
* In passive voice, the subject receives the action.
    * **EXAMPLE** - The burritos were eaten by me.

In the following sentences, identify if it is written in active or passive voice.

1. The sneaky thief negligently stole the rare jewels from the vault of the prestigious jewelry store.
   ....

2. The extravagant and lavish treasure was stolen by the ruffled pirates.
   ....

3. My cousin Joe greedily ate all of my Halloween candy and didn't ask.
   ....

4. The moldy cheese was eaten by the hungry rodents in the garage.
   ....

5. The vicious Chihuahua growled at the panicked mail carrier last Saturday.
   ....

6. The grandiose house on the corner was owned by my grandfather Bill.
   ....

7. Write your own sentence in active voice.
   ....

8. Write your own sentence in passive voice.
   ....

Week 2 Writing
Topic 3 Expressing Your Opinion

Through writing, you can express your opinion regarding important topics in this world. Brainstorm current news topics or community issues that are bothering you and ones that you would like to see changed.

1. What domestic or worldly issues and problems would you like to see changed in this world? These problems can be on a smaller scale, like problems at your school, or on a larger scale with problems happening in different countries. Make a list of five different problems.

    a. ....

    b. ....

    c. ....

    d. ....

    e. ....

2. Looking at your list, what is the most important problem that needs to be changed?

    ....

3. How should this issue be changed? What would you like to see happen?

    ....

4. What are your three reasons why this problem or issue needs to be solved?

    a. ....

    b. ....

    c. ....

Week 2 Math
Topic 5 Percent Problems

1. Mrs. Richards works at a furniture store where she makes 9% commission on all furniture she sells. If she sells $19,200 worth of furniture in April, how much commission will she make?

2. The sales tax in your city is 9.1% and an item costs $55 before tax. How much tax would you pay on that item? Round to the nearest hundredth or cent.

3. The sales tax in your city is 7.9% and an item costs $14 before tax. How much would you have to pay for the item after tax? Round to the nearest hundredth or cent.

4. A group of 4 friends go out for dinner and split the bill evenly. The total on the bill is $64 before tax. The tax rate is 9.5% and on top of this they tip 20%. How much does each person pay? Round to the nearest hundredth or cent.

5. A car salesman receives 1% commission on the total amount of all the cars he sells. If he sells $196,792 in cars for a month, what is his commission that month?

6. The total bill on your dinner at a fancy restaurant was $99.86 after tax. If you leave an 18% tip, what is the total after tip and tax?

FITNESS PLANET → Let's get some fitness in! Go to page 167 to try some fitness activities.

Week 2 Social Studies
Topic 1 — Italian Renaissance: Achievements in Art and Literature

1. Define Renaissance.

   ....

   During the period of the Renaissance, many artists began to change their artwork. Their artwork began to change and mimicked life. It focused on human beings and nature.

2. Look up paintings made during the Renaissance era in order to see examples of this change. What were some famous artists during this time period?

   a ....
   b ....
   c ....

   Many of the artists in the Renaissance era believed in humanism.

3. What is humanism?

   ....

4. Not only was art popular during the Renaissance, but so was literature. What three titles were written in the Renaissance Era? Use the Internet in order in order to answer.

   a ....
   b ....
   c ....

Grade 7-8
WEEK 3

It's time to train your brain for:

* adding/subtracting rational numbers
* points of view
* density, mass and volume
* atoms/chemical elements and more!

Week 3 Math
Topic 1 Add and Subtract Rational Numbers

1. $2.03 + 5.41 + 1.6 =$ ▢

2. $5\frac{1}{4} + 2\frac{2}{3} =$ ▢

3. $-3\frac{6}{7} + 2\frac{1}{5} =$ ▢

4. $-4.62 + 2.39 - 1.06 =$ ▢

5. $\frac{9}{2} - \frac{10}{3} =$ ▢

6. $-1.75 + 2\frac{5}{6} =$ ▢

Week 3　Math
Topic 2　Multiply and Divide Rational Numbers

1. $\dfrac{2}{7} \div 1\dfrac{5}{8} =$ ☐

2. $-9\dfrac{1}{2} \times 2\dfrac{1}{3} =$ ☐

3. $-1.43 \times 2.35 =$ ☐

4. $\dfrac{9.801}{-7.26} =$ ☐

5. $\dfrac{2}{5} \div \dfrac{1}{4} \div \dfrac{7}{10} =$ ☐

6. $1\dfrac{1}{7} \times \dfrac{1}{2} \div \left(-\dfrac{8}{5}\right) =$ ☐

FITNESS PLANET → Let's get some fitness in! Go to page 167 to try some fitness activities.

Week 3 Reading
Topic 1 Points of View

Key Vocabulary

* **First-Person Narration** - a character in the story that tells his or her first hand experience

    KEYWORDS - I, me, my, our, us, we, myself, ourselves

* **Second-Person Narration** - the reader is the character; often used in choose your own adventure stories.

    KEYWORDS - you

* **Third-Person Narration** - the narrator tells the story

    ■ There are three different categories of Third-Person Narration:

    ☐ Third-Person Objective
    - The narrator tells another person's story through the characters' actions and what they say through dialogue.

    ☐ Third-Person Limited
    - The narrator tells about one character's thoughts and feelings.

    ☐ Third-Person Omniscient
    - The narrator tells the inner workings of many characters.

        KEYWORDS - he, she, them, they, him, her, his, their

Week 3 Reading

Topic 1 Points of View

Read the following short paragraphs. Then, identify the point of view used.

1. Outside, it was raining oh so slightly. Aria and Jake were standing outside a small convenience store underneath the awning. They were trying to stay warm as the temperature dropped below thirty degrees and they were wearing shorts and short sleeved shirts. After waiting ten minutes, Jake said, "I told you to bring an umbrella." Aria replied, "I know, but I didn't think it was going to rain." They waited for ten more minutes and then decided to just walk home in the rain.

   What is the point of view in this passage? ....

   How do you know? Explain. ....

2. Outside, it was raining oh so slightly. Aria and Jake were standing outside a small convenience store underneath the awning. Aria could tell that Jake was really upset. After waiting for what seemed like an hour to Jake since he was so cold, he said, "I told you to bring an umbrella." Jake was really upset. He didn't want to get his new shirt all wet, especially when he had a job interview later that afternoon. Aria replied, "I know, but I didn't think it was going to rain."

   What is the point of view in this passage? ....

   How do you know? Explain. ....

3. Outside, it was raining oh so slightly. I was standing outside a small convenience store underneath the awning. My friend Jake and I were trying to stay warm because it was so cold. It dropped below thirty degrees and I was just wearing shorts and a t-shirt. Jake is mad at me because I forgot to bring an umbrella with us, but I really didn't think it was going to rain.

   What is the point of view in this passage? ....

   How do you know? Explain. ....

Week 3 Science

Topic 1 Density, Mass, and Volume

Identify the key terms below.

1. Density - ....
2. Mass - ....
3. Volume - ....

To calculate and know a missing calculation, use the equation below.

Density = mass / volume

Density equals mass divided by volume

Now you know the equation, calculate the missing numbers.

4. Mass is 39 and volume is 50. What is the density? ....

5. Mass is 15 and volume is 3. What is the density? ....

6. Mass is 70 and volume is 4. What is the density? ....

Week 3 Science
Topic 2 Atoms and Chemical Elements

1. What are atoms? ....
   ....

2. What is the center of an atom called? ....
   ....

3. The nucleus of the atom contains .... and ....
   ....

4. What are electrons? ....
   ....

5. Label the atom.

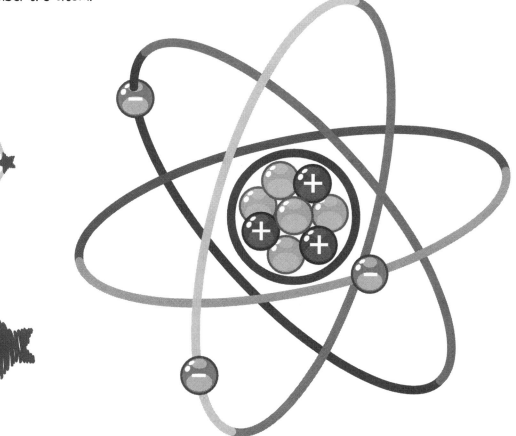

FITNESS PLANET → Let's get some fitness in! Go to page 167 to try some fitness activities.

43

Week 3 Math
Topic 3 Find the Missing Value

1. Use the number line to find the missing value: -3 + ☐ = 5

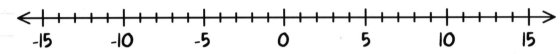

2. Use the number line to find the missing value: ☐ + (-3) = -5

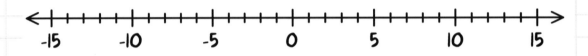

3. Use the number line to find the missing value: -1 - ☐ = -9

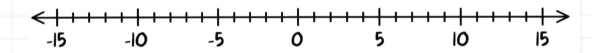

4. Use the number line to find the missing value: -8 - ☐ = -3

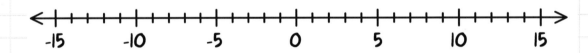

5. Use the number line to find the missing value: ☐ - (-10) = -5

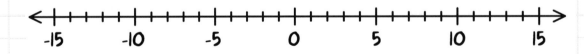

6. Use the number line to find the missing value: -9 = -5 + ☐

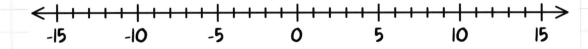

44

Week 3 Math
Topic 4　Simplify Complex Fractions

1. $\dfrac{2\frac{8}{9}}{4\frac{1}{3}} =$

2. $\dfrac{-\frac{3}{4}}{-\frac{5}{12}} =$

3. $\dfrac{1\frac{3}{4}}{\frac{2}{3}} =$

4. $\dfrac{\frac{11}{8}}{3\frac{1}{4}} =$

5. $\dfrac{-3\frac{1}{5}}{-\frac{1}{10}} =$

6. $\dfrac{\frac{9}{2}}{-6\frac{1}{3}} =$

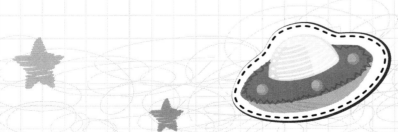

45

Week 3 Language
Topic 2 Moods

Key Vocabulary

* Indicative Mood - states facts
    * **EXAMPLE** - I was in that restaurant last year.
* Imperative Mood - makes a command or a request
    * **EXAMPLE** - I have to go to that restaurant.
* Subjunctive Mood - expresses a wish or a desire
    * **EXAMPLE** - If I went to that restaurant, I would eat so much sushi.
* Conditional Mood - shows a possibility
    * **EXAMPLE** - I may order sushi at that new restaurant.
* Interrogative Mood - asks a question
    * **EXAMPLE** - Did Jane go to that restaurant?

Read the sentences below. Then, indicate which mood the sentence is written in.

1. I got a perfect score on my midterm in world history class. ....

2. I have to attend summer school since I did poorly on the state standardized tests. ....

3. If Mrs. Jay postpones the math test to Monday, then I would have all weekend to study. ....

4. I may have to attend summer school if I don't improve my grades in math. ....

5. Did you get "John Adams" as an answer for number three in last night's homework? ....

6. I enjoy going to the zoo, but I usually feel bad for the animals that are locked up in their cages. ....

7. I have to stay at home on a Friday night and clean the entire house because my parents are having guests this weekend. ....

8. If my mother allows me to go to the movies with my friends, we are going to see the new *Frozen* movie. ....

9. I may go to the movies on Tuesday with my friends from soccer. ....

10. Do you want to go to the movies with me and my friends? ....

Week 3 Writing
Topic 3 Informative Writing

What is informative writing?

Informative writing covers a topic that the writer wants to research and learn more about. Let's jot down some ideas about an informative topic.

1. What topic do you want to learn more about? This can be a country or even an animal.

2. Now that you have picked your topic, go on the Internet and research. Write down three resources you have found. Make sure these resources are credible. These articles and scholarly journals should have an author and should be published within the last five years.

   a. ....

   b. ....

   c. ....

3. Now that you have read resources about your topic, write down important facts you have learned about your topic.

   a. ....

   b. ....

   c. ....

   d. ....

   e. ....

 FITNESS PLANET → Let's get some fitness in! Go to page 167 to try some fitness activities.

Week 3 Math
Topic 5 Number Line Operations

1. Write an expression that describes the following: On a number line, start at -3 and move 5 units to the left.

2. Write an expression that describes the following: On a number line, start at -8 and move 4 units to the right.

3. Is $a + b$ negative or positive?

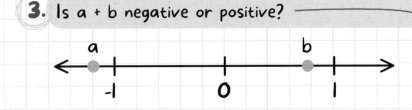

4. Is $c - (-d)$ negative or positive?

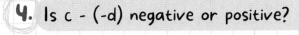

5. Is $-f + e$ negative or positive?

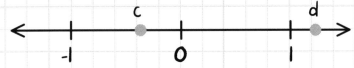

6. Is $g - h$ negative or positive?

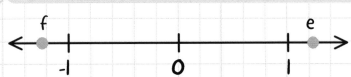

Week 3 Social Studies
Topic 1 The Louisiana Purchase

Read information about the Louisiana Purchase. Then, answer the questions that follow.

In the early 1800s, the colonists used the Mississippi River as a transportation hub to trade goods; however, they were not allowed to use New Orleans, which at that time was not part of the United States. Many wanted to go to war with France in order to obtain it, but Jefferson did not think that was a good idea. Instead, he petitioned to buy a chunk of land that included New Orleans.

In the year 1803, the government purchased land from France for fifteen million dollars. This transaction is known as the Louisiana Purchase. This purchase, made by the United States government and steer headed by President Thomas Jefferson, was beneficial because it doubled the size of the land that the United States owned. The land that was purchased was west of the Mississippi River and east of the Rocky mountains.

This purchase cost the government fifteen million dollars, which breaks down to three cents per acre. In our world today, an acre costs around a thousand dollars. This area was beneficial for the country to purchase not only due to New Orleans, but also due to being near the Mississippi river, having rich soil in the area, and a vast number of trees.

1. Why do you think Jefferson didn't want to go to war against France to obtain New Orleans?

   ....
   ....

2. How was this purchase a "good deal"?

   ....
   ....

3. What were the benefits of this land? Why did the United States government want land with these qualities?

   ....
   ....

Grade 7-8
WEEK 4

Get ready for a new adventure with:
- negative numbers
- verbal shifts
- chemical structure
- central idea and more!

Week 4 Math
Topic 1 Add & Subtract Negative Numbers

1. $6 - 3 - (-3)$ →
2. $-10 + 2 - (-6)$ →
3. $-5 + 4 - 3 + (-1)$ →
4. $-7 - (-10) - (-12)$ →
5. $-3 - 2 - 1 + (-6)$ →
6. $-8 - (-9) + 9 - 1$ →

FITNESS PLANET → Let's get some fitness in! Go to page 167 to try some fitness activities.

Week 4 Math
Topic 2 Multiply & Divide Negative Numbers

1. $0 \div (-12)$ →

2. $-9 \times (-6)$ →

3. $-11 \div 0$ →

4. $-8 \times 2 \div (-4)$ →

5. $14 \div (-7) \times (-5)$ →

6. $-12 \div (-3) \div (-2)$ →

Week 4 Language Review
Topic 1 Verbal Shifts

Writers need to be careful and make sure that the verbs match the same tense when used in the same sentence. Sometimes, the first verb does not match the second verb. This can be confusing for the reader.

Read the following sentences, then edit the verbs to match the first.

1. Mario drank the milk so fast that he gets stomach pains and nausea.

2. Angelia completed her science homework; however, she did not gotten them all correct and receives a failing grade.

3. When my mother and I arrived at the fancy restaurant, my dad is eating.

4. On the day of my soccer game, the sun was shining and the birds are singing.

5. My grandfather receives a hunting magazine every month but he barley ever read it.

6. My little sister screams when my mother put her on Santa's lap.

53

Week 4 Writing

Topic 1 Analyzing Both Sides Of An Issue

Should students be required to wear uniforms in school?

In persuasive writing, it is important to look at both sides of an issue, regardless of what you believe. Looking at the question, research both sides of the issue.

Claim: Students should be required to wear school uniforms.

1. What three resources did you find regarding this claim?

   a. ....
   b. ....
   c. ....

2. What three reasons back up this claim?

   a. ....
   b. ....
   c. ....

Claim: Students should not be required to wear school uniforms.

3. What three resources did you find regarding this claim?

   a. ....
   b. ....
   c. ....

4. What three reasons back up this claim?

   a. ....
   b. ....
   c. ....

5. Which side would you choose to write about in a persuasive essay? Why did you choose this side?

   ....

Week 4 Science
Topic 1 Chemical Structure

A chemical's structure is how the atoms are arranged in a substance.

1. What is a reactant? ....
   ....

2. What is a product? ....
   ....

There are different characteristics of a chemical's structure. Define those characteristics.

3. Melting Point ....
   ....

4. Density ....
   ....

5. Solubility ....
   ....

 FITNESS PLANET → Let's get some fitness in! Go to page 167 to try some fitness activities.

55

Week 4 Science
Topic 1 Chemical Structure

To see how chemical structure comes into play, follow the experimental protocol below.

Materials Needed:

- 150 grams of coconut oil
- Skillet
- Deep pan
- 36 grams of hydrogen peroxide
- 30 grams of water

Steps:

- Mix 36 grams of hydrogen peroxide and 30 grams of water
- Heat the 150 grams of coconut oil to 120 degrees
- Pour the coconut oil into the hydrogen and water mixture
- Blend for five minutes
- The soap will begin to get thicker
- Pour the mixture into a mold
- Tap to remove the air bubbles

 What did you learn from this experiment?

 Using the above terms, explain the process of making soap in your own words?

Week 4 Math

Topic 3 — Convert Fractions to Decimals and Decimals to Fractions

1. Rewrite $\frac{17}{10}$ as a decimal.

2. Rewrite 7.72 as a mixed number in simplest form.

3. Rewrite $\frac{18}{5}$ as a decimal.

4. Rewrite 10.02 as a mixed number in simplest form.

5. Rewrite $\frac{10}{3}$ as a decimal.

6. Rewrite 3.95 as a mixed number in simplest form.

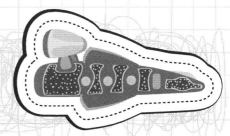

Week 4 Math

Topic 4 Real-World Problems Using Rational Numbers

1. At the grocery store, you spent $5 on apples. The apples cost $1.25 per pound. How many pounds of apples did you buy?

2. You spent $32 on a taxi including a $2 tip. The taxi cost is $2.50 per mile. How many miles did you travel?

3. Your car uses 1 gallon of gasoline for every 18 miles driven. Gasoline costs $2.50 per gallon. You're taking a road trip travelling 432 miles and your gas tank holds 12 gallons. How many times will you have to fill up your tank? How much will gas cost?

4. Frances took a ride home from the airport in a shuttle with her 7 friends. The cost of the shuttle was $93 total, plus they tipped $5. How much did Frances pay if they split the cost evenly?

5. The price of oats in the bulk section at the grocery store is $0.99 per pound. The price of a 5-pound box of oats is $6.29. How much less expensive is it to buy 5 pounds of oats in the bulk section than buying a 5-pound box of oats?

6. Hailey and Callie are practicing swimming to the bottom of the pool. Hailey is 5.6 feet below the surface of the water. Callie is 1.3 feet above Hailey. What is Callie's position relative to the surface of the water?

Week 4 Reading
Topic 3 Finding the Central Idea in NonFiction

Read the nonfiction passage below. Then, answer the questions that follow.

Some very common animal myths and old wise tales have been dictated to us as young children and have even been written in children's books for many years. These sayings include how all elephants are extremely frightened of mice, that ostriches stick their heads in the ground to drink water, and that dogs and cats despise each other and will never ever get along. Whether or not there is some validity to these myths, they are common.

Have you ever heard the saying that you are as blind as a bat? This is a saying that people may jokingly blurt out if you can't see something or if you are holding a book very close to your eye. Where in the world did this saying come from? Is it a myth; or are bats really blind?

This famous and familiar saying can easily be proven wrong by a recent scientific study conducted by Purdue University, which is located in Lafayette, Indiana. Professors and students wanted to test their theory in order to see whether or not bats were really blind.

For this particular experiment, the science professors used the assistance of lightning bugs to conduct their theory. For quite some time now, animal trainers, bat experts, and scientists have known that bats do not enjoy the taste of lightning bugs. They are not sure if lightning bugs are too salty or maybe just too bitter for them; but nonetheless, lightning bugs are not a chosen delicacy by bats.

Using this information about a bat's diet, the professors blacked-out the bottom portion of three hundred lightning bugs with non-lethal paint so that the lightning bugs would not cast off their normal yellow glow. Then, the experimenters let the bats out to feed. They immediately flew to the lightning bugs, ate them, and spit them out. This first showed the scientists that maybe bats were blind because they flew to a well-known insect they did not like to eat; however, their study was far from over. The next day, the scientists let the bats out again, this time they released regularly lit lightning bugs amongst the bats. Surprisingly, the bats remembered from the past that lightning bugs were disgusting; so they saw their light, remembered it, and avoided them as they associated it to the past, thus proving that bats have strong enough eyesight to see the lightning bugs' light.

FITNESS PLANET → Let's get some fitness in! Go to page 167 to try some fitness activities.

Week 4 Reading

Topic 3 Finding the Central Idea in NonFiction

1. What is the central idea of this passage?

2. What are three supporting details that support the central idea?

3. What is the author's purpose in this article?

4. Write a summary of the nonfiction article.

Week 4 Math
Topic 5 Ordering Rational Numbers

1. Put the following numbers in order from least to greatest:

   $\frac{7}{6}$, 1.2, $1\frac{9}{35}$ →

2. Put the following numbers in order from least to greatest:

   $\frac{41}{10}$, 4.05, $4\frac{1}{3}$ →

3. Put the following numbers in order from least to greatest:

   -2.9, $-2\frac{3}{8}$, $-\frac{11}{4}$ →

4. Put the following numbers in order from least to greatest:

   -3.1, $-3\frac{1}{5}$, -2.99 →

5. Circle all numbers that are less than -1.125:

   $-\frac{9}{8}$, -0.125, $-1\frac{2}{5}$, 1.2, $-1\frac{4}{9}$, 0

6. Circle all numbers that are greater than -2.75:

   0, -1.5, -2.95, $-\frac{5}{2}$, $-2\frac{8}{9}$, $-\frac{8}{3}$

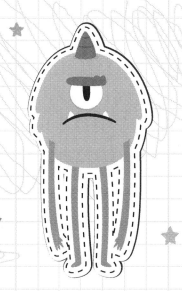

Week 4 — Social Studies
Topic 1 — The U.S. - Mexican War

The U.S.-Mexican War or otherwise known as the Mexican-American War occurred between 1846 and 1848. During this time, many individuals had strong feelings about Manifest Destiny.

1. What is Manifest Destiny?
   ....

2. What are some positive benefits of this mentality?
   ....

3. What are some negative outcomes of this mentality?
   ....

The United States government at this time, under the presidency of James K. Polk, believed in Manifest Destiny. After Polk became elected, the United States annexed the state of Texas.

4. What does the word "annexed" mean?
   ....

This action was a major reason why the U.S.-Mexican War started. Mexico warned the United States government that war would be inevitable if Texas was annexed. The two countries could not agree on where the border of Mexico ended and the United States started. This then led to the beginning of the war in 1846 when Polk sent troops into Texas.

5. Do you think that the United States should have annexed Texas? Explain.
   ....

Grade 7-8
WEEK 5

Now let's learn about:

- linear expressions
- archetypes
- velocity, distance and time
- equivalent expressions
- and more!

Week 5   Math
Topic 1   Add & Subtract Linear Expressions

1. Simplify:
   $(2x - 3) + (-x - 7)$

2. Simplify:
   $(3x^2 + 4x - 1) - (x - 10)$

3. Simplify:
   $(7 - 9x) - (10 - 2x)$

4. Simplify:
   $(a + 7b) + (3a - 11b)$

5. Simplify:
   $(7j^2 + 3j - 2) - (9j^2 + 4j - 1)$

6. Simplify:
   $(9m + 4) + (5m^2 - 8m + 2)$

Week 5 Math
Topic 2 Expand Linear Expressions

1. Expand and combine like terms:
$3x(9x^2 - 5x)$

2. Expand and combine like terms:
$-2(7u - 11)$

3. Expand and combine like terms:
$(x + 7)(x^2 + x - 1)$

4. Expand and combine like terms:
$(a^2 - 4a + 9)(-a)$

5. Expand and combine like terms:
$-8x(y^2 - y + 1)$

6. Expand and combine like terms:
$(7a - 1)(9a + 2)$

FITNESS PLANET → Let's get some fitness in! Go to page 167 to try some fitness activities.

Week 5 Reading

Topic 1 Archetypes in Fiction

What is an archetype?

An archetype is a recurrent symbol or example that occurs in many stories. Archetypes can be present in characters, setting, conflict, and the theme.

Read the story below. Then, answer the questions that follow.

The Anklet For A Princess: A Cinderella Story From India

Public Domain Material

Once upon a time, in Eastern India, a girl named Cinduri worked extremely hard every day. Three times a day, she balanced a heavy pot on her head to gather drinking water for her family. She also had to clean the house, prepare the meals, and milk the cows every day. Last year, an epidemic of cholera swept through her entire village. Her father had died of the disease, and she had no mother as she died earlier from the same disease. This left Cinduri to stay with her father's second wife and her daughter named Lata. The didn't love Cinduri and they often treated her badly. At night, Cinduri prayed to her godfather in order to help her and show her some love. Cinduri's godfather told her that the Crown Prince was coming to their village to celebrate the Navaratri Festival. Cinduri's stepmother would not allow her to attend the festival. When Cinduri tried to leave their hut, Cinduri's stepmother ripped Cinduri's silver anklet off of her left foot and instead put it on Lata's ankle since it was so beautiful. That anklet belonged to Cinduri's mother.

That evening, when Cinduri finished all of her chores, Cinduri summoned her godfather. He told her to turn in a circle. Cinduri did and at first she felt a bit silly. Then she began spinning faster and faster. Her old rags magically turned into the purest golden threads. Magnificent jewels appeared in her hair. She had two of the most beautiful anklets she had ever seen around her ankles. They were decorated with tiny bells and covered with diamonds that sparkled in the moonlight. The godfather told Cinduri to go to the festival, but that she needed to return home at midnight as the magic will disperse.

At the festival, the Crown Prince had eyes only for her, and together, they danced all night. Then when midnight came around, the Prince was going to ask Cinduri to marry him; however, he couldn't find her. All he found was one tiny bell. The Prince was determined to marry the girl with the bell. He sent messengers all over the village to find the girl with the missing bell.

The Prince's messenger arrived at Cinduri's hut. The stepmother made Cinduri keep busy with her chores. The messenger looked at Lata's anklet, but it didn't even have any bells even though she was lying and saying it did. As the messenger was about to leave, he saw a pretty girl in the barn milking the cows. She immediately showed him her beautiful anklet adorned with twenty bells, with one missing. The messenger immediately took Cinduri to the castle to meet the Prince. When the Prince saw Cinduri, he proclaimed "This beautiful princess is my bride!"

Week 5　Reading

Topic 1　Archetypes in Fiction

1. Who is the archetypal hero character in this story? Explain.
....
....

2. Who is the archetypal mentor in this story? Explain.
....

3. What is the archetypal setting in the story? Explain
....

4. What is the archetypal conflict in the story? Explain.
....

5. Who is the archetypal villain character in the story? Explain.
....
....

Week 5 Science

Topic 1 Velocity, Distance, and Time

Identify the terms below.

1. Velocity - ....

2. Distance - ....

3. Time - ....

Speed is how fast or slow something is moving; the speed of the car, the speed of the elderly couple on the sidewalk, and the speed of the snail moving up the side of the flower pot.

To calculate speed, the equation is below.

Speed = distance ÷ time

Speed equals distance divided by time.

FITNESS PLANET → Let's get some fitness in! Go to page 167 to try some fitness activities.

Week 5 Science
Topic 1 Velocity, Distance, and Time

Let's practice.

4. If a turtle is covering a distance of 12 inches and it takes him 5 minutes to do so, what is the turtle's speed?

....
....
....

5. If a woman is jogging around a track for a distance of 1200 meters and it takes her ten minutes to do so, what is the woman's speed?

....
....
....

6. If a lion chases after an antelope in the prairie for 400 yards and it takes him 12 seconds, what is the lion's speed?

....
....
....

7. Now, create your own question in order to calculate speed, then find the answer to your own question.

....
....
....

Week 5 Math
Topic 3 Equivalent Expressions

1. Are the expressions 2x + 2 and 2(x + 2) equivalent?

2. Are the expressions -5x - 5 and -5(x + 1) equivalent?

3. Are the expressions 8a and 8(a + 1) equivalent?

4. Are the expressions $\frac{12}{a}$ and $12(\frac{1}{a})$ equivalent?

5. Are the expressions $2x^2 + 2x + 2$ and $2x(x^2 + x + 1)$ equqivalent?

6. Are the expressions 7ab + a and a(7b + 0) equivalent?

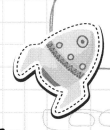

Week 5 Math
Topic 4 Powers

1. Rewrite in the form x^n: $(x^7)^3$.

2. Rewrite in the form 10^n: $(10^4)^7$.

3. Solve for x: $(a^4)^5 = a^x$.

4. Rewrite in the form g^n: $\dfrac{g^5}{g^3}$.

5. Rewrite in the form h^n: $\dfrac{(h^3)^2}{h^5}$.

6. Rewrite in the form b^n: $\dfrac{(b \times b \times b \times b \times b \times b \times b)}{(b \times b \times b)}$.

Week 5 Language
Topic 2 Using Punctuation To Indicate Pauses

Key Vocabulary

* An ellipsis is three dots . . .
  * Ellipses are used when text is left out or when there is a pause in dialogue or thought.

* A dash is indicated by this symbol -
  * Dashes are used to focus on special information in a sentence and to indicate an interruption in the text.

In the sentences below, explain why the punctuation is used and how it is helpful.

1. According to the article "Reasons Why Students Should Not Wear Uniforms", Matt Rauscher notes "The National Center for Education Statistics reports that . . . school uniforms reduce crime rates in public schools by forty five percent" (Rauscher 1).

   ....
   ....

2. Mia was presenting her project to the class. Mia explained, "Alexander Hamilton was . . . a . . . influential leader in this country."

   ....
   ....

3. Derek was trying to multitask. He was rushing to school and grabbed his phone to text his mother to tell her that —. That was the last thing Derek remembered before he woke up in the hospital.

   ....
   ....

Week 5 Writing

Topic 3 Outlining An Argument

Outline an argument in order to prepare yourself to write an argumentative essay. Refer back to the previous question, "Should school uniforms be mandatory for public school children?"

1. What is your claim?
   ....

2. What are your three reasons and what are your subpoints in each reason?

   a. Reason One - ....
      - I Subpoint One - ....
      - II Subpoint Two - ....
      - III Subpoint Three - ....

   b. Reason Two - ....
      - I Subpoint One - ....
      - II Subpoint Two - ....
      - III Subpoint Three - ....

   c. Reason Three - ....
      - I Subpoint One - ....
      - II Subpoint Two - ....
      - III Subpoint Three - ....

 FITNESS PLANET → Let's get some fitness in! Go to page 167 to try some fitness activities.

Week 5 Math
Topic 5 One-Step Inequalities

1. Solve $8x < 10$

2. Solve $\frac{1}{2}y > -2$

3. Solve $x + 8 \geq 5$

4. Solve $11 \leq c - 9$

5. Solve $\frac{d}{4} > 2$

6. Solve $12f < 36$

Week 5 Social Studies
Topic 1 Northern and Central America

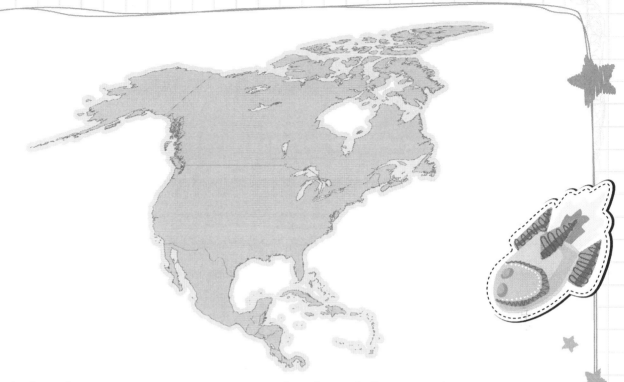

Label the following countries in North and Central America

* Bahamas
* Barbados
* Belize
* Canada
* Costa Rica
* Cuba
* Dominican Republic
* El Salvador
* Guatemala
* Haiti
* Honduras
* Jamaica
* Mexico
* Nicaragua
* Panama
* Trinidad and Tobago
* United States of America

Next to each country, write an interesting fact that you learned about it after researching on the Internet.

Grade 7-8
WEEK 6

It's time to show what you know about:

* two-step equations
* informative essay
* plant cells
* purposes of government and more!

Week 6 Math
Topic 1 Two-Step Equations

1. Solve for m:
$3m + 6 = 19$

2. Solve for h:
$23 - h = 11h$

3. Solve for y:
$6 - \frac{1}{5}y = 10$

4. Solve for x:
$3x = 8x - 4$

5. Solve for j:
$9j = 2j - 14$

6. Solve for a:
$-a + 6 = a + 10$

FITNESS PLANET → Let's get some fitness in! Go to page 167 to try some fitness activities.

Week 6 Math

Topic 2 Two-Step Equation Word Problems

1. A taxi charges a flat fee of $5 plus $3 per mile. Your last taxi ride cost $29. Write an equation to determine the number of miles traveled on this taxi ride. Then solve the equation.

2. The price of gasoline went up $0.21 per gallon. Gina bought 6 gallons of gasoline for $17.52. Write an equation to determine the original price per gallon, p.

3. A rectangle has a perimeter of 52 cm and a side length of 15 cm. Write an equation to determine the width, w, of the rectangle. Then solve the equation.

4. Each chicken on the farm hatches 6 eggs per week. The farmer decides to sell 8 chickens. His remaining chickens hatch a total of 204 eggs the next week. Write an equation to determine how many chickens he had originally.

5. A rectangular storage shed has a length that is twice its width. The perimeter of the shed is 105 feet. Write an equation that can be used to find the length and width. Then solve the equation to find the dimensions of the shed.

6. You spent $1,950 on new furniture. The local furniture store allows you to make a down payment of $600 and then pay the remaining balance in 6 equal monthly payments. Write an equation that can be used to find the amount of each payment, p. Then solve the equation to find the amount of each monthly payment.

Week 6 Writing
Topic 1 Sources

How are sources written in MLA format?

First let's find sources for an informative topic. Research a city you would like to learn more about.

1. What city will you be researching?
   ....

2. Find three sources regarding your topic?

   a. ....

   b. ....

   c. ....

Now, let's pull some direct evidence from the articles and properly cite the information you have found. Remember that a signal phrase is needed before direct quotes. Then, after the direct quote, the period is removed and placed after the parenthesis. Inside the parenthesis is the author's last name. If there is no author, the article or source is used.

Here is an example:

According to the Encyclopedia Britannica, "Tokyo was formerly called Edo until the year 1868" (Encyclopedia Britannica).

3. In the sources, write down three pieces of evidence and properly cite the evidence used.

   a. ....

   b. ....

   c. ....

Week 6 Writing
Topic 2 Informative Essay

Informative writing explains more information on a topic. It includes what you want to learn more about and what you want to teach your readers about.

Let's focus on a disease for this informative outline.

1. What disease do you want to research? ....

2. What resources did you find regarding your topic?

   a. ....

   b. ....

   c. ....

3. What are your three topics or body paragraphs and your subpoints in your informative essay?

   a. Point 1 - ....

      I Subpoint 1 - ....

      II Subpoint 2 - ....

      III Suppoint 3 - ....

   b. Point 2 - ....

      I Subpoint 1 - ....

      II Subpoint 2 - ....

      III Suppoint 3 - ....

   c. Point 3 - ....

      I Subpoint 1 - ....

      II Subpoint 2 - ....

      III Suppoint 3 - ....

Week 6 Science

Topic 1 Functions of the Plant Cell

Match the parts of the plant cell to its function.

1. chloroplasts ....
2. rough endoplasmic reticulum ....
3. smooth endoplasmic reticulum ....
4. nucleus ....
5. lysosome ....
6. mitochondria ....
7. vacuole ....
8. ribosome ....
9. cell wall ....
10. cytoplasm ....
11. cell membrane ....

a. Aids in photosynthesis

b. Rigid outside layer; protects and supports the cell

c. Semi-permeable; regulates what comes in and out

d. Stores DNA

e. Made up of RNA and protein

f. Provides energy to the cell

g. Digestive organ

h. Produces proteins

i. Makes hormones and lipids

j. Breaks down waste

k. Maintains pressure in the cell

 **FITNESS PLANET** → Let's get some fitness in! Go to page 167 to try some fitness activities.

81

Week 6 Science
Topic 1 Functions of the Plant Cell

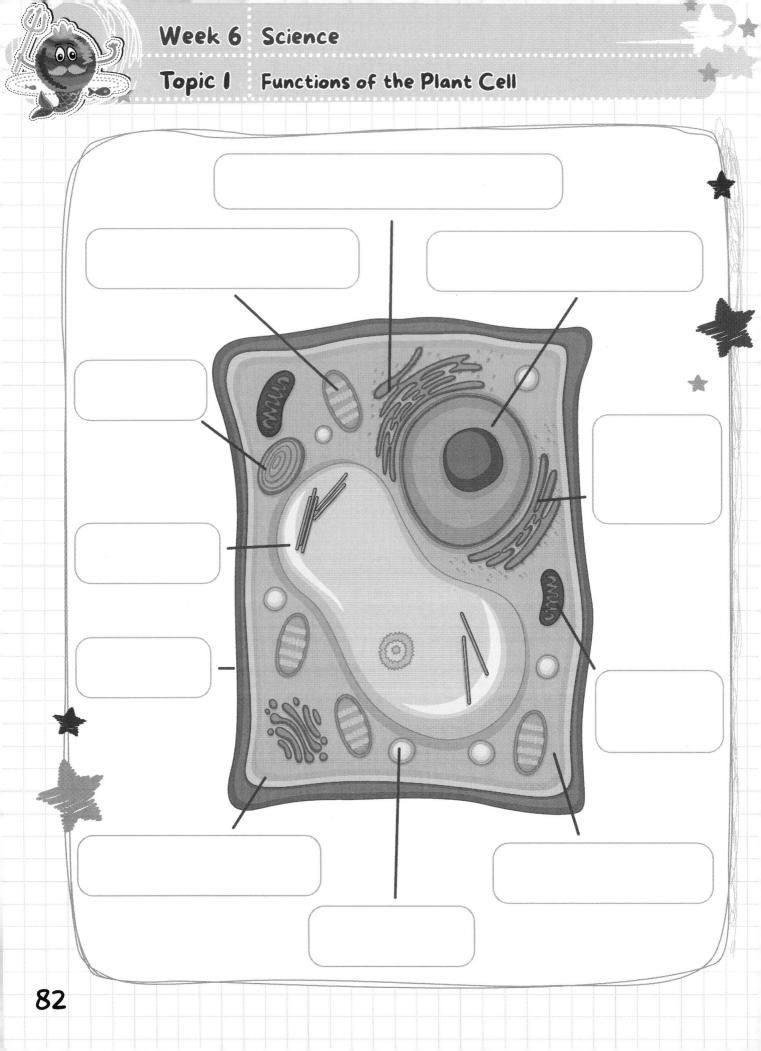

Week 6 Math
Topic 3 — Two-Step Equations with Decimals and Fractions

1. Solve:
$1.5y = 3y + 4.5$

2. Solve:
$\dfrac{4}{5}x + \dfrac{7}{2} = \dfrac{1}{5}x$

3. Solve:
$0.8a + 9 = 1.7a$

4. Solve:
$\dfrac{2}{3}p = \dfrac{1}{2}p + 3$

5. Solve:
$10.5j = 8.1j - 6$

6. Solve:
$1 + \dfrac{9}{4}u = \dfrac{1}{8}u$

Week 6 Math
Topic 4 Two-Step Inequalities

1. Solve:
$7y - 3 < 11$

2. Solve:
$-9 \geq 4x + 3$

3. Solve:
$5 - 6b > 14b$

4. Solve:
$\frac{t}{2} + 1 \leq 5$

5. Solve:
$10 < -\frac{j}{2} + 6$

6. Solve:
$k > 4k + 7$

Week 6 Reading
Topic 3 Comparing Points of View

Read the two passages, then answer the questions that follow.

Passage 1

Malala Yousafzai was born in 1997 in the country of Pakistan. As a young child, Malala thoroughly enjoyed attending school each day. She loved reading about far away adventures and journeys. Reading helps Malala get her mind off of her difficult life. Malala lives in a war torn country, leaving her and her family to worry about safety on a daily basis. Malala could not attend school in her town, as that school was designated for boys only. Malala begged her parents to allow her to attend the closest school for girls, which was many miles away from their home. Malala's parents knew that Malala loved to learn and valued education, so they paid a fee to allow Malala to ride on their version of a school bus, which is an open cart driven by horses. Even though Malala was on her school bus for a long time, she never complained because she loved attending school.

On October 9th, 2012, when Malala was just fifteen years old, she boarded the school bus like any normal day; however, this day was anything but normal. As Malala and her classmates were on the school bus, it was stopped by the Taliban, which is a dangerous group in Malala's country. The Taliban did not believe that girls should attend school.

Malala and two other females were shot by a member of the Taliban. A bullet hit Malala's head. Even though this is a fatal injury, Malala lived with the help of medical professionals. After recovering from her injury, Malala spoke all over the world about the importance of education. She also speaks out against the rules on education in her country. Through her bravery and her passion to help others learn, Malala was the youngest person to receive the Nobel Peace prize.

Passage 2

My name is Malala and I was born in 1997 in the country of Pakistan. Growing up, I loved going to school and I loved to read. My favorite stories were fairy tales and stories based on history. I loved learning about the past. Reading took my mind off of the fighting in the streets. Even though the local school for girls is miles away from my home, I didn't care because I loved attending school and I loved learning.

On October 9th, 2012, when I was fifteen years old, the day started off like any normal day. I was on the bus headed to school. My friends and I were chatting. All of a sudden, the bus was stopped by the Taliban, which is a dangerous group in my country. The Taliban did not like it that girls like me were attending school.

I was shot by a member of the Taliban. A bullet hit my head, but thankfully, with the help of medical professionals, I lived. I strived to survive because it is important to stand up to the Taliban. It is important that everyone gets the right to attend school, even girls.

Let's get some fitness in! Go to page 167 to try some fitness activities.

Week 6 Reading
Topic 3 Comparing Points of View

1. What point of view is passage one written in? ....
   ....
   ....

2. What keywords were used? ....
   ....
   ....

3. What point of view is passage two written in? ....
   ....
   ....

4. What keywords were used? ....
   ....
   ....

5. How are the passages similar? ....
   ....
   ....

6. How are the passages different? ....
   ....
   ....

7. Which passage did you like better? Explain. ....
   ....
   ....
   ....
   ....
   ....

Week 6 Math

Topic 5   Two-Step Inequality Word Problems

1. A bakery spends $105 on supplies once a month and $128 daily on expenses. Write an inequality you could use to find the minimum monthly income, i, the bakery must earn to break even if there are n days in a month. Solve the inequality if there are 30 days in the month.

2. Timothy has $20 to spend at the movie theater. The movie ticket costs $14 and snacks are $2 each. Write an inequality you could use to find the maximum number of snacks, s, Timothy can buy. Solve the inequality.

3. The school is doing a fundraiser at a local facility that costs $500 to rent for the day. Tickets cost $12 each. Write an inequality that you could use to find how many tickets they need to sell if they want to raise at least $800. Solve the inequality.

4. A college student receives a grant to cover part of his tuition and living expenses. The total grant is $5000 for the semester. He will use $3000 for tuition. He plans to withdraw $125 each week for living expenses. How many weeks can he withdraw $125? Write and solve an inequality.

5. Two-thirds of a number plus 5 is greater than 12. Write an inequality that could be used to find the number. Solve the inequality.

6. You spend $15 to buy supplies for the bake sale. You bake 50 cookies. How much should you charge per cookie so that you end up making a profit of at least $25 at the sale? Write and solve an inequality.

Week 6 Social Studies
Topic 1 Purposes of Government

Our government is in place for many different reasons. Some of the purposes are listed below.

Explain what each purpose entails.

1. To keep order
   ....

2. What is an example of this purpose?
   ....

3. What would happen if this purpose was not in place?
   ....

4. To protect
   ....

5. What is an example of this purpose?
   ....

6. What would happen if this purpose was not in place?
   ....

7. To provide public services
   ....

8. What is an example of this purpose?
   ....

9. What would happen if this purpose was not in place?
   ....

FITNESS PLANET → Let's get some fitness in! Go to page 167 to try some fitness activities.

Grade 7-8
WEEK 7

Let's go on an adventure with:
- decimals
- word roots
- figurative language
- climate regions and more!

Week 7 Math
Topic 1 Scale Drawings

1. A scale on a travel map shows that 0.5 inch represents 10 miles. What number of inches on the map represent 45 actual miles?

2. A scale drawing of a house uses a scale of $\frac{1}{4}$ inch to represent 1 foot. The drawing shows the house will be 4.5 inches long on one side. How many feet long will that side of the house be?

3. A scale on a world map shows that 250 miles is represented by 1.25 inches. Australia is about 12.5 inches wide on the map. How many miles wide is the actual continent of Australia?

4. Your teacher asks you to construct a scale drawing of the Eifel Tower, which is 984 feet tall not including the tip. If your scale is 1.5":144', how tall should your drawing be?

5. The distance between your town and the next town is 140 miles. On the map of your two towns, the scale is 3 cm represents 20 miles. How many centimeters apart are the towns on the map?

6. Town A and Town B are 6 inches apart on the map. Town B and Town C are 5.5 inches apart on the map. The map has a scale of 1 inch to 25 miles. How many miles closer is Town B to Town C than it is to Town A?

Week 7 Math

Topic 2 Construct Scale Drawings

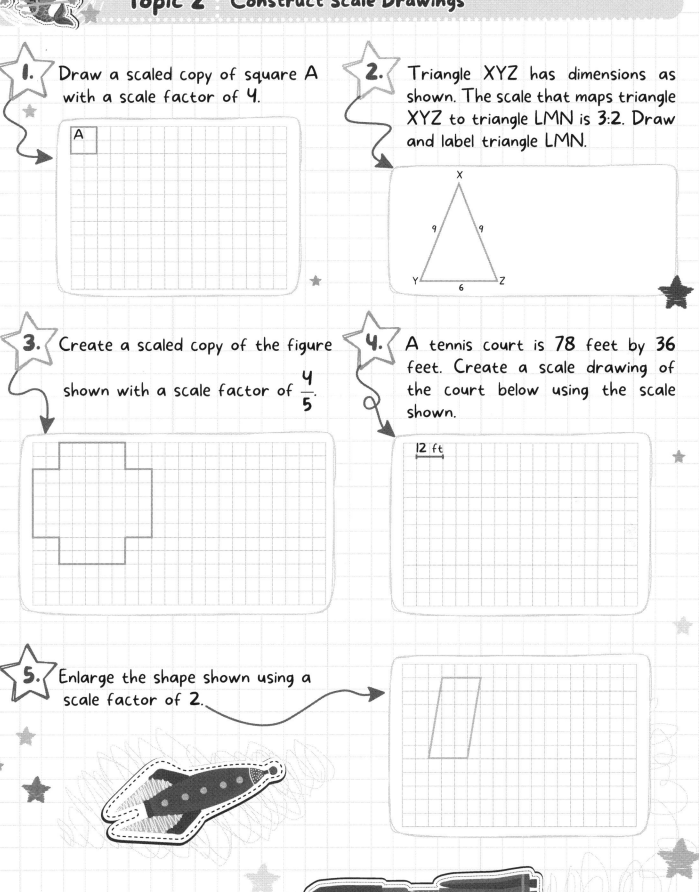

1. Draw a scaled copy of square A with a scale factor of 4.

2. Triangle XYZ has dimensions as shown. The scale that maps triangle XYZ to triangle LMN is 3:2. Draw and label triangle LMN.

3. Create a scaled copy of the figure shown with a scale factor of $\frac{4}{5}$.

4. A tennis court is 78 feet by 36 feet. Create a scale drawing of the court below using the scale shown.

5. Enlarge the shape shown using a scale factor of 2.

Week 7 Language
Topic 1 Context Clues

Context clues are needed when there are difficult words that are hard to identify. Read the short passages below, then identify the difficult vocabulary words using the surrounding context clues.

1. Desiree found **solace** in her novels. When she had horrible days at the office, she would go home, grab a blanket, make herself a cup of hot cocoa, relax in her comfy recliner, and settle down to read one of her mystery novels. These novels take Desiree away from her hectic life into far off lands of mystery and adventure.

   What does the word **solace** mean? ....
   ....

   Which context clues led you to make this decision? ....
   ....

2. My uncle Ernie **abhorred** laziness. He has lived and worked on a farm his entire life. He gets up at four o'clock in the morning, feeds the horses and the chickens, milks the cows, and tends to the sheep. If that was not enough, he tends to the crops until the late hours of the night. When we go visit, he doesn't like for us to sit and watch TV or play video games, he wants us out helping him.

   What does the word **abhorred** mean? ....
   ....

   Which context clues led you to make this decision? ....
   ....

FITNESS PLANET → Let's get some fitness in! Go to page 167 to try some fitness activities.

Week 7 Language
Topic 1 Context Clues

3. The judge **rebuked** the defendant for being rude in his courtroom. He was talking when others were talking, even after the judge warned him several times. He also used swear words and elbowed the bailiff. She rebuked him.

    What does the word **rebuked** mean? ....
    ....

    Which context clues led you to make this decision? ....
    ....

4. The thieves **surmised** that the Smiths were not home. They observed their house for several days and didn't see anyone coming or going. Since it snowed, they checked for tracks, and the freshly new snow was unmoved in the driveway. The mail also seeping out of the mailbox.

    What does the word **surmised** mean? ....
    ....

    Which context clues led you to make this decision? ....
    ....

Week 7 Science
Topic 1 Functions of the Animal Cell

Match the parts of the animal cell to its function.

1. cell membrane ....
2. cytoplasm ....
3. nucleus ....
4. rough endoplasmic reticulum ....
5. smooth endoplasmic reticulum ....
6. ribosomes ....
7. golgi apparatus ....
8. lysosomes ....
9. mitochondria ....
10. vacuoles ....

a. Where the organelles are housed
b. Digestive organ
c. Transportation system; contains Ribosomes
d. Protects and offers stability to the cell
e. Temporarily stores protein
f. Powerhouse of the cell
g. Produce proteins
h. Stores food, water, and waste
i. Transportation system; does not contain Ribosomes
j. Control center of the cell

Week 7 Science

Topic 1 Functions of the Animal Cell

Next, label the animal cell below.

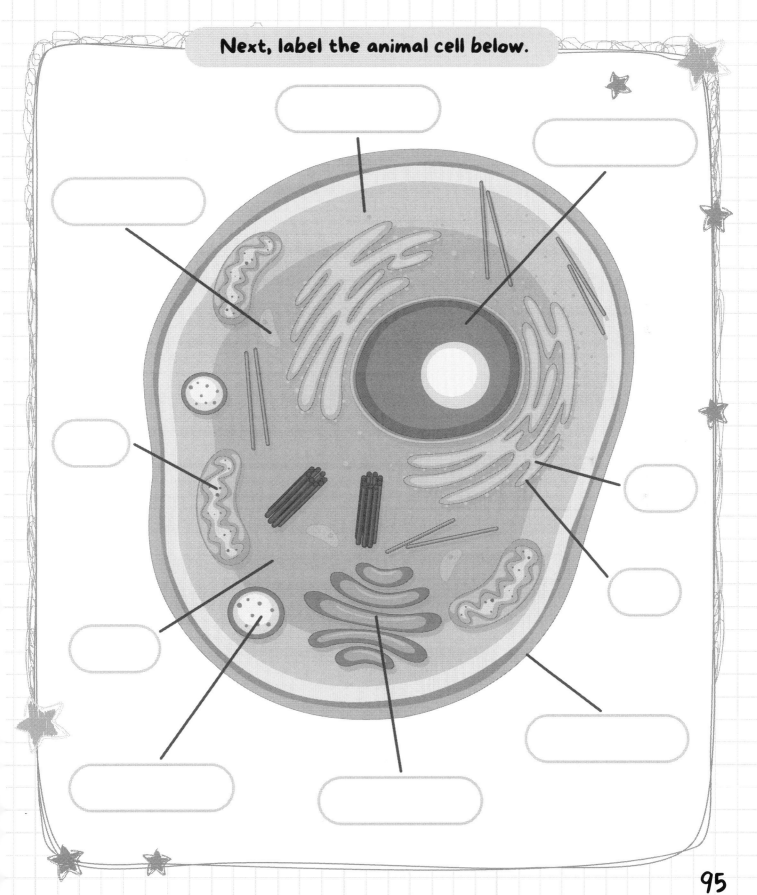

Week 7 Math
Topic 3 Identify Scale Factor

1. Figure A is a square with side lengths 1.25 mm. Figure B is a square with side lengths 5 mm. What is the scale factor from figure A to figure B?

2. Figure Y is a scaled copy of figure Z. What is the scale factor from figure Z to figure Y?

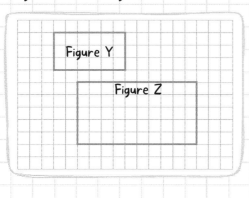

3. A house is 22 feet tall. The scale drawing of the house shows its height is 12 inches. What is the scale factor from the drawing to the house?

4. Figure J is a scaled copy of figure K. What is the scale factor from figure K to figure J?

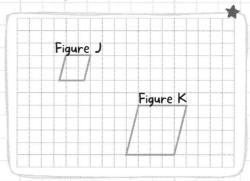

5. ABCDE is a scaled copy of LMNOP. What is the scale factor from ABCDE to LMNOP?

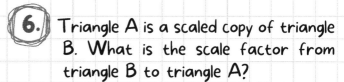

6. Triangle A is a scaled copy of triangle B. What is the scale factor from triangle B to triangle A?

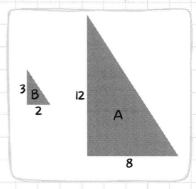

Week 7 Math

Topic 4 Triangle Side Lengths and Pythagorean Theorem

1. Could 2, 3 and 7 be the side lengths of a triangle?

....

....

2. Could 6, 6, and 1 be the side lengths of a triangle?

....

....

3. Why is it not possible to construct a triangle with side lengths 1, 2 and 3?

....

....

4. Find the missing side of the right triangle.

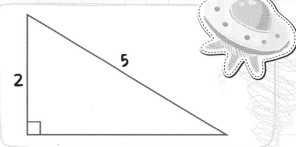

....

5. Find the missing side of the right triangle.

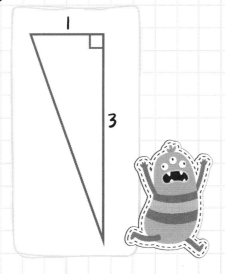

6. A wheelchair ramp must have a ratio of 1:12 for its slope. If you are constructing a wheelchair ramp that is 2 feet high, how long should the ramp be? Round to the nearest thousandth.

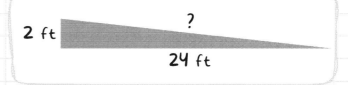

....

Let's get some fitness in! Go to page 167 to try some fitness activities.

Week 7 Reading
Topic 2 Using Textual Evidence in Fiction

Read the fictional passage below. Then, answer the questions that follow.

Excerpt from Chapter One "The Old Sea-dog at the Admiral Benbow" in *Treasure Island* by Robert Louis Stevenson

Public Domain Material

Dr. Livesey and the rest of the important gentlemen propositioned me to write down the entire particulars about the illustrious Treasure Island adventure. They desire to know the entire story from the very beginning to the bitter end. They don't want me to hold back any details, only the detailed information regarding the bearings of the island because there is still treasure not yet lifted there.

I eagerly take up my pen and mentally go back to the time when my father kept the Admiral Benbow Inn, as this is the moment when everything started. A dirty old seaman, called the stranger, with a sabre cut directly across the center of his leather face first took up his lodging under our roof. I remember him as if it were only yesterday. He came plodding up the rocky road to the inn door, his sea-chest bumping behind him on a thick and long brown rope. The stranger was a tall, strong, and heavy man. His tarry pigtail fell over the shoulder of his soiled and torn blue coat. His hands ragged and scarred, with black and broken nails. I remember him looking around the inn nervously and whistling to himself. That whistle was piercing, eerie, and distinct.

The stranger did not have the appearance of a man that rode the mast, although he did say he was from the sea and spent his entire life there. Thinking back on the stranger, I remember that he was a very silent man by custom. All day he hung around the cove in silence, parading back and forth as if he were searching or waiting for something. All evening he sat in a corner of the parlor next to the fire, again as if he were waiting for something long overdue. The stranger would not speak when spoken to, only looked up suddenly and fiercely.

And that was all I could ever learn of our guest.

1. Come up with three adjectives that describe the stranger. Use textual evidence to support your claims. ....
....

2. How does the narrator feel about the stranger? Use textual evidence to support your claims. ....
....

3. Why is the narrator describing the stranger? Infer why his description is important? Use textual evidence to support your claims. ....
....

Week 7 Writing
Topic 3 Signal Shifts

Authors use signal shifts and transitional wording to show their audience that time has passed, as well as when the setting changes. If an author misses these signal shifts, then the audience will be confused about when and where the story is occuring.

Read the short examples below. Then, write a paragraph or two about the situation, making sure to add signal shifts to indicate a passing of time and a change in setting.

1. A little girl named Suzie hits another little girl named Amaya at recess. The recess monitor tells Suzie's teacher, Mrs. Gooden. Suzie's teacher, Mrs. Gooden, converses with Suzie about her behavior. She sends Suzie to Mr. Terry, the principal. Mr. Terry talks with Suzie about her behavior. Mr. Terry gives Suzie an after school detention for hitting. She has to serve her detention the following day.

2. Erin has to get her wisdom teeth out on Tuesday at 8:00am. On Tuesday at 7:30, Erin arrives at Bright Smiles and checks in. She lays back in the chair and the nursing assistant numbs the area. The dentist, Dr. Routch, gives her a shot so she doesn't feel anything. Dr. Routch removes Erin's four wisdom teeth. At 9:15, Erin wakes up. She is very groggy and does not remember anything. Erin's mom takes her home and puts her to bed. At 6:30pm, Erin wakes up and she is in a lot of pain.

Week 7   Math
Topic 5   Plane Sections of 3D Figures

1. What two-dimensional shape is produced when this cylinder is sliced horizontally?

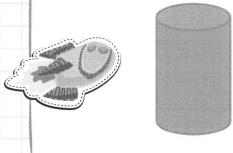

....

2. What two-dimensional shape is produced when this prism is sliced vertically?

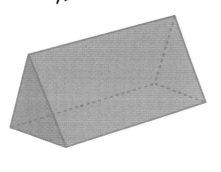

....

3. What two-dimensional shape is produced when this prism is sliced vertically?

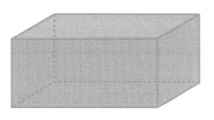

....

4. What two-dimensional shape is produced when a square pyramid is sliced horizontally?

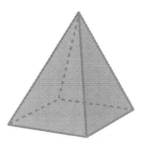

....

5. What two-dimensional shape is produced when this triangular prism is sliced horizontally?

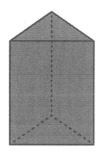

....

6. What two-dimensional shape is produced when this cylinder is sliced vertically?

....

Week 7   Social Studies
Topic 1   South America

Let's learn about South America! If you need help with some of these questions, ask an adult or use the Internet to learn about South America.

1. The Americas are grouped into four regions. Name them:
   a. ....
   b. ....
   c. ....
   d. ....

2. Did you know that South America is the fourth largest continent. Which continents are bigger?
   a. ....
   b. ....
   c. ....

3. What is the most spoken language in South America? ....

4. South America has many tepuis. What are they? ....
   ....

5. What imaginary line runs through the top of South America? ....

6. What imaginary line runs through the middle of South America? ....

7. Research South America and discover five facts about the region.
   a. ....
   b. ....
   c. ....
   d. ....
   e. ....

 FITNESS PLANET → Let's get some fitness in! Go to page 167 to try some fitness activities.

Grade 7-8
WEEK 8

Let's see how well you know:

* radius and diameter
* advanced root words
* the rock cycle
* nonfiction paragraph structure and more!

Week 8 Math

Topic 1 Radius and Diameter

1. What is the radius of the circle?

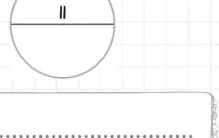

....

2. What is the diameter of the circle shown?

....

3. True or False: The diameter of a circle is always twice the radius.

....

4. The circumference of a circle is 9π cm. What is the radius of the circle?

....

5. The area of a circle is 36π square meters. What is the diameter of the circle?

....

6. The diameter of a circle is x. What is the radius of the circle?

....

Week 8 Math
Topic 2 Area of a Circle

1. Find the area of a circle with radius 12 ft.

....

....

2. Find the area of a circle with diameter 18 centimeters.

....

....

3. Find the area of a circle with radius 2y.

....

....

4. The area of circle A is 49π square mm. The area of circle B is 81π square mm. How much bigger is the diameter of circle B than the diameter of circle A?

....

....

5. Find the area of the shaded region of this circle.

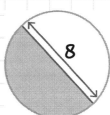

....

....

6. Find the area of the shaded region of this circle.

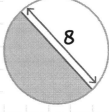

....

....

FITNESS PLANET → Let's get some fitness in! Go to page 167 to try some fitness activities.

Week 8 Language

Topic 1   Advanced Root Words

Below is a list of important root words that 8th graders need to know. Write three words that contain that root word. Then, pick one word and write an original sentence using that word.

1. Cred - to believe

   .... , ... , ...

   ....

2. Belli - war

   .... , ... , ...

   ....

3. Crat or Cracy - rule, strength, or power

   .... , ... , ...

   ....

4. Hemo or Hema - blood

   .... , ... , ...

   ....

5. Mar - sea

   .... , ... , ...

   ....

6. Pel - to drive or push

   .... , ... , ...

   ....

Week 8 Writing
Topic 2 Transitions

Transitional words and phrases help writers connect their ideas and shows their audience what happens next. In the sentences below, add transitional wording and more content that connects with the initial sentences.

1. My father used his outdoor fryer to cook the Thanksgiving turkey.

2. Our family arrived at the airport two hours early for our flight to the Bahamas.

3. The store owner counted the money in the register at the end of the day and realized that three hundred dollars was missing.

4. My brother was the winner of the trivia contest at work and won home tickets to the Lakers.

5. My left back tire is flat.

In the sentences below, the transitional word or words are missing. Please fill in the missing transitional word or words in the sentences.

6. The lead actor was late due to a car accident, ... the opening performance of *Hamilton* was delayed.

7. .... I read the directions and followed every single step, the shelf I put together opens backwards.

8. Sue Ellen left school late because she was getting math help from her teacher. ...., back at Sue Ellen's apartment, her mother was worried that she was not home.

9. Elliot thought he was the best basketball player at his entire school; ...., he didn't make the basketball team this year.

10. When searing a steak, you .... need to get the skillet hot before adding the oil.

Week 8 Science
Topic 1 The Rock Cycle

> Did you know that minerals make up rocks and a rock can be composed of more than one mineral?

Here are the properties of rocks:

* Solid form
* Natural
* Not living

Here are the properties of minerals:

* Solid form
* Natural
* Not living
* Pure
* Fixed crystal structure

Rocks and minerals have similar properties; however, rocks are not pure as they are composed of different substances and they do not have a fixed crystalized structure. A fixed crystalized structure explains that the atoms are always positioned in the same manner.

Week 8 Science
Topic 1 The Rock Cycle

What is Joey holding?

1. Joey is holding something in his hand. He is not sure if he is holding on to a rock or a mineral. It is in solid form and it is weighing down his pocket. Joey knows that what he is holding isn't or hasn't ever been alive. It is gray and has a striped pattern. His dad told him that it is not pure.

   What is Joey holding in his hands?
   ....

2. In the rock cycle, rocks continuously change forms and are shaped into new rocks through many different processes.

   There are three main types of rock. Define them. Then, identify the process that creates them.

   * Igneous rocks - ....
     * Igneous rocks are formed through a process called ....

   * Metamorphic rocks - ....
     * Metamorphic rocks are formed through the process called ....

   * Sedimentary rocks - ....
     * Sedimentary rocks are formed through the process called ....

Week 8 Math
Topic 3 Circumference of a Circle

1. Find the circumference of a circle with diameter 10 ft.

2. Find the circumference of a circle with radius 6 inches.

3. The circumference of a circle is 81π mm. What is the radius of the circle?

4. The circumference of a circle is 1.5π m. What is the diameter of the circle?

5. Find the arc length of the partial circle.

0.5 in

6. Find the arc length of the semicircle.

6 ft

FITNESS PLANET → Let's get some fitness in! Go to page 167 to try some fitness activities.

Week 8 Math
Topic 4 Complementary, Supplementary & Vertical Angles

1. Find the complement of 72°.

2. Find the supplement of 72°.

3. Find the complement of b°.

4. Find the supplement of b°.

5. Find x

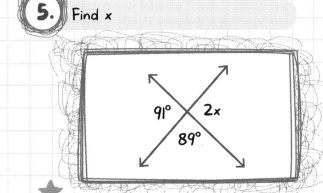

6. Find a.

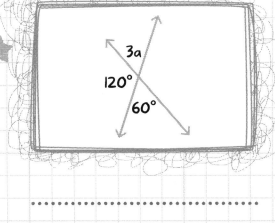

Week 8 Reading

Topic 3 Nonfiction Paragraph Structure

Read the nonfiction passage below.
Then, answer the questions that follow.

(1) Scientists have been working hard to find other planets in and out of our galaxy that may be equipped for human visitors in the future. Astronomers and scientists have found that a planet just outside of our solar system can potentially hold life. This newly discovered planet is called K2-18b and has temperatures that are ideal for humans and are similar to the temperatures on Earth. K2-18b is not extremely hot or cold like other planets in our solar system. Water vapor has also been found on this new planet, which is located just outside the Leo star system.

(2) Having the ideal temperature as well as water is what humans need to survive, but scientists are not ready to send humans there on a spaceship just yet. They still need to conduct more research to determine if this far off planet is an ideal environment for humans. Scientists are in constant research to see if they can find other planets with sustainability, and this is a good first step.

(3) The K2-18b planet is double the size of Earth and is very rocky. Its sun is cooler and smaller than ours. It also has a different atmosphere than what we have on Earth. K2-18b takes around thirty-three days to circle its sun, so our year is equal to their month. Their sun is red and gives off radiation, and may not be healthy for humans.

Week 8 Reading

Topic 3 Nonfiction Paragraph Structure

1. What is the thesis statement or claim in this passage?
   ....
   ....

2. Write one sentence that supports this claim.
   ....
   ....

3. Write another sentence that supports this claim.
   ....
   ....

4. What is the purpose of passage 1?
   ....
   ....
   ....

5. What is the purpose of paragraph 2?
   ....
   ....
   ....

6. What is the purpose of paragraph 3?
   ....
   ....
   ....

Week 8 Math
Topic 5 Transformations

1. Plot point A' which is the translation of point A 4 units down and 2 units to the right.

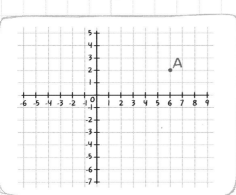

2. Plot point B', which is point B reflected across the x-axis.

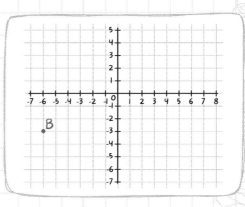

3. Reflect triangle XYZ over the line g.

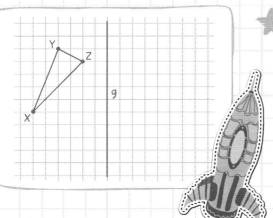

4. Circle all aspects of a figure that don't change during a rotation or translation:

A. The area of the figure
B. The coordinates of the vertices of the figure
C. The angle measures in the figure
D. The shape of the figure

5. Rectangle ABCD is rotated 270° about a point to create rectangle A'B'C'D'. If the measure of AB is 5 units, what is the measure of A'B'?

....

....

6. Translate triangle XYZ 3 units down and 5 to the right.

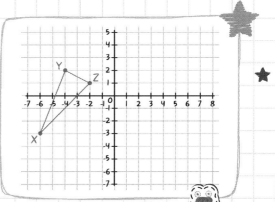

FITNESS PLANET → Let's get some fitness in! Go to page 167 to try some fitness activities.

Week 8 Social Studies

Topic 1   The French and Indian War

Read the passage below. Then, answer the questions that follow.

The French and Indian War did not take place in India or France, but instead, this war happened in North America during the 1750s and 1760s. The French and Indian War was a small part of a much larger war called The Seven Years War that involved many different continents. The French and Indian War was also a catalyst to the American Revolution that occurred later in history.

The reason this war began was that many different countries wanted to rule the land in North America. England and France wanted to claim the North American land as their own and they fought over who would own it. At that time prior to the war, the English land was known as the Thirteen Colonies and the French land was known as New France. As many English and French citizens began settling, their land grew, and their land started touching. This had the two countries fighting over what land they claimed. The two countries fought over the land which is west of the Appalachian Mountains and the land in the Ohio River Valley. This land had rich soil, which was strong for farming and producing food. This land also gave access to the Native Americans, which traded many goods with them like food and fur.

During the time before the war, 1740, there were more British settlers than French settlers. The British thought that it would be easy to get the French off of "their" land. The British decided to send George Washinton over to the French land and give them a message to tell France to vacate their land in the Ohio River Valley. The French told Washington that they were not leaving and it was "their" land.

This then led Geroge Washinton to gather a small troop to fight the French; however, the French gathered more troops and the small British troop was outnumbered. George Washington and his troops surrendered. This initial fight caused the French to prepare and the British to get more troops. This also caused the Native Americans to worry about their land and they started to take sides based on who they traded with.

At this time, Ben Franklin wanted all the thirteen colonies to join together and fight as one. He wanted the thirteen colonies to fight as one united government. In 1755, Great Britain sent many troops to the thirteen colonies and France sent many French soldiers to their land. This is when the fight initiated and when Britain declared war on France. Many soldiers died during this war, but the British won.

1. What the main idea of this historic passage?
   ....
   ....

2. Summarize the events that led to the French and Indian War?
   ....
   ....

Grade 7-8
WEEK 9

Get ready to master:

- random samples
- themes
- ecosystems
- probability models and more!

Week 9 Math

Topic 1 Making Inferences from Random Samples

1. The school surveyed a sample of 120 students asking how many times each week they planned to buy lunch from the cafeteria. 46 students said 2 or less times per week, 54 students said 3 times per week, and the remaining students said 4 or 5 times per week. Based on these results, how many of the 500 students in the entire school would you expect to buy lunch in the cafeteria 3 times next week?

2. The city randomly sampled some of its population to determine which type of store to put in the empty space on Main Street. Here are the results:

Type of Store	Number of Votes
Bakery	21
Restaurant	35
Retail - home	36
Retail - clothing	8

Based on the results, how many of the city's 2500 residents would prefer a restaurant in the empty space on Main Street?

3. John took a random sample of 30 students from his school and asked them what their favorite dessert was. 18 students said cake was their favorite dessert. There are 450 students in John's school. Use his results to estimate how many students in the school would choose cake as their favorite dessert.

4. A company surveyed a random sample of 54 of its employees asking whether they would take a trip or stay home during their vacation time. 18 employees said they would take a trip. Based on these results, how many of the company's 1200 employees would you expect to take a trip during their vacation time?

5. A vacuum company surveyed a random sample of 152 people likely to buy vacuums, asking what type of vacuum they were most likely to buy. 38 said they would prefer a cordless vacuum. The company will make 50,000 vacuums this year. Based on these results, how many cordless vacuums should they make?

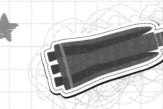

Week 9   Math

Topic 2   Making Inferences about Two Populations

1. The first dotplot shows the test scores of Mrs. Jameson's first period math class. The second dot plot shows the test scores of Mrs. Jameson's last period math class. Is it clear that one class had higher overall test scores? If so, which one?

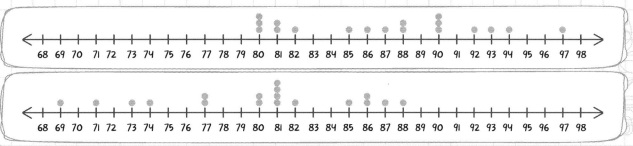

2. The histograms show the number of calories consumed by participants in a study on dieting. What piece of information can be gathered from these histograms?

A. The participants in group 1 ate more calories on average.
B. The participants in group 2 ate more calories on average.
C. None of the above.

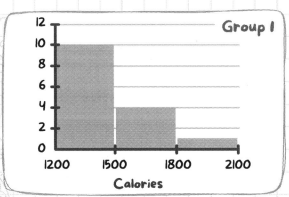

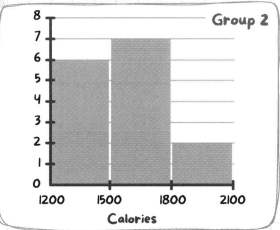

3. The boxplots show the heights (in inches) of freshman and senior boys at a high school. What piece of information can be gathered from these boxplots?

A. All the seniors are taller than all the freshmen.
B. The seniors are taller than the freshmen in general.
C. None of the above.

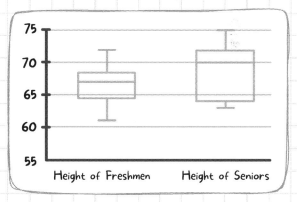

4. True or False: If population A has a higher average salary than population B, that means everyone in population A earns more money than everyone in population B.

117

Week 9 Reading
Topic 1 Theme

Read the following fictional story. Then, answer the questions that follow.

Excerpt from Chapter 5 "Advice From the Caterpillar"
in *Alice's Adventures in Wonderland* by Lewis Carroll

Public Domain Material

Alice found herself in another strange location as she was eye to eye with a talking and rather rude Caterpillar. Alice began to feel frustrated because the Caterpillar never answered any of her questions. After what seemed to Alice like an eternity, she finally decided to turn away from him as the Caterpillar was being extremely rude and she didn't have the patience for him any longer.

As Alice was angrily rushing away from him, the Caterpillar boisterously yelled out for her to come back. He explained to her that he had something very important to tell her. Alice quickly thought that this was promising news, so she turned around and went back to where the Caterpillar was standing. When Alice reached the Caterpillar, he leaned in as if he was going to tell her something important. He then told Alice that she needs to learn to keep her temper.

Alice was infuriated by his comment because she did not think that was important news at all. Alice held back her welling tears and explained to the Caterpillar that she was not feeling herself today. She was tired of changing sizes and she just wanted to be normal. One moment she was quite small, and the next, she was gigantic and larger than a house.

After staring at her for some time, the Caterpillar told Alice that the dilemma was quite easy to resolve. He explained to her that one side of the magical mushroom would make her grow taller and the other side of the magical mushroom would make her grow shorter. However, the Caterpillar never told Alice which side was which before he scurried away from her and escaped into a pile of brown mushy leaves. Alice looked thoughtfully at the mushroom for quite some time, trying to make out which side was which.

  Let's get some fitness in! Go to page 167 to try some fitness activities.

Week 9　Reading
Topic 1　Theme

1. What is the definition of the word theme?

2. What is the theme of this passage?

3. How does Alice and the Caterpillar develop the theme in this passage?

4. How does the setting of Wonderland help develop the theme in this passage?

5. How does the conflict of the Caterpillar not giving Alice direct advice help develop the theme in this passage?

Week 9 Science

Topic 1: Structure and Function of Organic Compound Groups

1. What are organic compounds? ....

   There are four groups of organic compounds. Explain their function.

2. Carbohydrates - ....

   a. What three elements are carbohydrates composed of? ....

   b. What is the smallest form of carbohydrates called? ....

3. Lipids - ....

   a. What is an example of a lipid? ....

4. Proteins - ....

   a. What are the building blocks of protein called? ....

5. Nucleic Acids - ....

   a. What is an example of a nucleic acid? ....

Week 9 Science
Topic 2 Ecosystems

Ecosystems are biological communities that have similar organisms and a similar climate. This includes both biotic and abiotic elements.

Ecosystems have three main categories:
* Climate
* Types of soil
* Different organisms that reside there

Read the descriptions of different ecosystems below. Then, in the lines provided, describe which organisms live there and give an example of a location of that particular ecosystem.

* **Cold Desert Ecosystems**
    * Small amounts of rain or snow
    * Thin soil
    * Long cold winters

Organisms - ....

Location - ....

* **Temperate Deciduous Forest Ecosystems**
    * Warm and wet summers, cold and wet winters
    * Rich soil
    * Lush forests; but not many different types

Organisms - ....

Location - ....

* **Taiga Ecosystems**
    * Long cold winters and short cool summers
    * Lush evergreen trees
    * Poor soil

Organisms - ....

Location - ....

* **Prairie Grassland Ecosystems**
    * Cool winters and hot summers
    * Lots of rainfall
    * Rich soil

Organisms - ....

Location - ....

* **Savanna Grassland**
    * Warm summers and winters
    * Rainy in winters and dry in summers
    * Poor soil

Organisms - ....

Location - ....

* **Hot Desert Ecosystems**
    * Little rain
    * Thin, dry soil
    * Many different organisms

Organisms - ....

Location - ....

Week 9 Math
Topic 3 Probability Models

1. You are randomly choosing a t-shirt out of a drawer containing different colored shirts. The following table shows the probability of choosing each color of shirt.

T-shirt Color	Probability
Gray	?
Blue	0.2
White	0.4
Black	0.3

What is the probability of choosing a gray shirt out of the drawer?

2. Bob counted the color of each car driving down his street for an hour. He counted 11 silver cars, 8 white cars, 6 black cars, 2 red cars and 3 green cars. Fill in the chart recording the probability of seeing each color car. Write your answer as a fraction or decimal rounded to the nearest hundredth.

Color Car	Probability
Silver	
White	
Black	
Red	
Green	

3. The farm store has different types of chickens for sale. On Saturday they sell 3 Rhode Island Red chickens, 5 Plymouth Rock chickens, 10 Ameracauna chickens, 3 Leghorn chickens and 2 Orpington chickens. They randomly select one of the chickens sold to give its owner a free bag of feed. What is the probability they randomly select a Plymouth Rock chicken?

4. You are playing checkers with a friend. Exactly one person will win each game. The probability that he will win is 0.35. What is the probability that you will win?

5. The weather forecast shows a 40% chance of rain tomorrow. What is the probability that it will not rain tomorrow?

6. Jen has baked 25 cakes. 5 of the cakes fell in the middle, 6 were underbaked, 2 were overbaked and the remaining were perfect. Based on these results, what is the probability that the next cake Jen bakes is perfect?

Week 9 Math

Topic 4 Approximating Probability of a Chance Event

1. You roll a 6-sided die once. What is the probability of rolling an even number?

2. You roll a 10-sided die once. What is the probability of rolling a number greater than 7?

4. Find the probability of spinning the spinner below and landing on yellow.

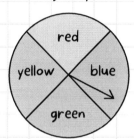

3. You choose a card from a deck of cards where half the cards are black and half are red. What is the probability of choosing a red card?

5. A random number generator has an equal probability of generating any integer from 1-20. What is the probability of randomly generating an integer less than 5?

6. A deck of cards contains 20 blue cards, 40 red cards, 15 yellow cards and 25 green cards. What is the probability of randomly choosing a yellow card from the deck?

FITNESS PLANET → Let's get some fitness in! Go to page 167 to try some fitness activities.

123

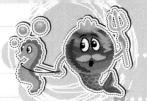

Week 9 Language
Topic 2 Use Reference Materials

Are you familiar with using a dictionary or a thesaurus?

A **dictionary** provides a lot more information than just a word's definition and a **thesaurus** gives you information about synonyms and antonyms. It is important to become familiar with using a dictionary and a thesaurus when writing in order to find more information about words and to see if a particular word fits into the sentence you are using.

Use a dictionary and a thesaurus to answer the following questions.

1. What is the definition of the word *ambiguous*?

2. Find three synonyms for the word *ambiguous*.

3. What is the definition of the word *assimilate*?

4. Find three synonyms for the word *assimilate*.

5. What is the definition of the word *rebuke*?

6. Find three antonyms for the word *rebuke*.

7. What is the definition of the word *boycott*?

8. Find three antonyms for the word *boycott*.

9. What part of speech is the word *imminent*? Use it in a sentence.

10. What part of speech is the word *theory*? Use it in a sentence.

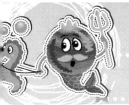

Week 9 Writing
Topic 3 Creating A Setting

Authors focus on describing a setting in their work in order to make their audience picture the scene in their minds. Practice describing a setting.

1. Describe the room you are currently in. ....
   ....

Authors often use sensory details to describe a setting. This makes the scene come alive. Sensory details include all five senses which are hearing, seeing, touching, tasting, and smelling.

2. Go back to the setting that you described above. Now, add sensory details to that description.
   ....

3. Now imagine that you are writing a mystery novel. Using sensory details and the room that you are currently in, describe your setting as if it were part of a criminal investigation.
   ....
   ....
   ....
   ....

Week 9 Math
Topic 5 Experimental Probability

1. A worker at an ice cream shop records the number of each flavor of ice cream sold on a Saturday. Based on her results, what is the probability the next person orders chocolate ice cream?

Ice Cream Flavor	Number Sold
Vanilla	21
Chocolate	9
Strawberry	5
Mint Chocolate Chip	15
Cookie Dough	18
Coffee	7

2. Millie drew 24 pictures in preschool. She always drew either trees, flowers, cats or dogs. The table shows the number of each type of picture she drew. Her dad randomly selects one picture to display in his office. What is the probability he will select a picture of dogs?

Picture	Number
Trees	3
Flowers	7
Cats	5
Dogs	9

3. Ashley receives the following scores on her history tests this year: 5 A's, 2 B's and 1 C. She randomly picks one test to show her parents. What is the probability she randomly picks the test she scored a C?

4. Every day Mr.Chip starts his class with a quiz, review question, or discussion. The students kept track and he has given a quiz 12 days, asked a review question 28 days and started with discussion 15 days. What is the probability that the next day he will start class with a quiz?

5. The last 10 cars sold by the car company were the following types: 3 SUVs, 2 minivans, 2 coupes and 3 trucks. What is the probability that the next car sold is a minivan?

6. A t-shirt company inspects its t-shirts after production. There were 4 defective t-shirts in the last 125 shirts they inspected. What is the probability the next t-shirt that comes to inspection is defective?

Week 9 Social Studies
Topic 1 Primary and Secondary Sources

In many of your classes in school, including history, you will read many different texts including primary and secondary sources.

A **primary source** is a first-hand retelling of what happened during that particular time period.

A **secondary source** is a second-hand retelling of what happened after that particular time period.

Let's practice identifying primary and secondary resources. Identify the type of source and then explain why it is that type of source.

1. A pamphlet that was given out during John F. Kennedy's election in 1960.

   Type of Source - ....
   Explanation - ....

2. A book written by a professor at New York University entitled "The Renaissance: The Beginning to the End."

   Type of Source - ....
   Explanation - ....

3. A map made by cartographers in 1901 to show where troops were in the South African War.

   Type of Source - ....
   Explanation - ....

4. A map that you purchased at the gas station.

   Type of Source - ....
   Explanation - ....

5. A memoir about Oprah Winfrey written by a famous author.

   Type of Source - ....
   Explanation - ....

6. A diary written by a World War II soldier.

   Type of Source - ....
   Explanation - ....

Grade 7-8
WEEK 10

Now let's work hard on:

* comparing probabilities
* scatter plots
* verbal irony and puns
* author's purpose and more!

Week 10   Math

Topic 1   Comparing Probabilities

1. The probability of event A is $\frac{1}{9}$ and the probability of event B is 0.1. Which event is more likely to occur?

2. Which has a greater probability: rolling an odd number on a 6-sided die or flipping a coin and it landing heads up?

3. A deck of cards contains 20 blue cards, 40 red cards, 15 yellow cards and 25 green cards. Which color card has the greatest chance of being randomly selected from the deck?

4. Lynn determined that the probability she will be at school on time if she leaves at 8:05 is 60% while the probability she will be at school on time if she leaves at 7:55 is 0.8. At which time should she leave to have the greatest probability of arriving on time?

5. Gerald flips a coin 100 times and 45 of these are heads up and 55 of them are tails up. How does his experimental probability of tossing a coin and having it land heads up compare to the theoretical probability of tossing a coin and having it land heads up?

6. A meteorologist determines that the probability a hurricane will hit land in Florida is 0.25. He also determines the probability this hurricane will hit land in Louisiana is 0.2. Is it more likely the hurricane will hit land in Florida or Louisiana?

FITNESS PLANET → Let's get some fitness in! Go to page 167 to try some fitness activities.

Week 10 Math
Topic 2 Scatter Plots

1. The scatter plot shows the salary earned and number of years worked for 9 employees at a company. What type of association is there between these variables?

A. Employees with more years of experience tend to earn higher salaries.
B. Employees with more years of experience tend to earn lower salaries.
C. There is no clear relationship between years of experience and salary.

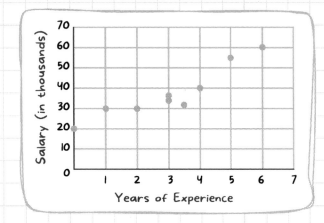

2. What type of association is shown in the scatter plot below?

A. Positive linear association
B. Negative linear association
C. Nonlinear association
D. No association

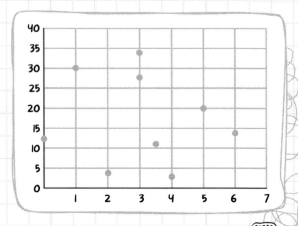

3. What type of association is shown in the scatter plot below?

A. Positive linear association
B. Negative linear association
C. Nonlinear association
D. No association

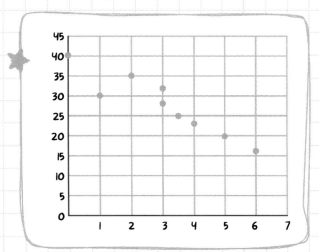

4. What type of association is shown in the scatter plot below?

A. Positive linear association
B. Negative linear association
C. Nonlinear association
D. No association

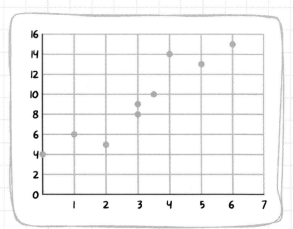

Week 10 Language

Topic 1 Verbal Irony and Puns

Key Vocabulary

- **Verbal irony** - saying something that is the opposite of what is expected; sarcasm
  - **EXAMPLE** - After eating a horrible meal, my mother said, "Well that was tasty."
- **Pun** - a joke made which uses the definition of words
  - **EXAMPLE** - The shy turtle is really starting to come out of its shell.

VERBAL IRONY

Underline the verbal irony used in the following sentences. Then, explain why that is an example of verbal irony.

1. My math teacher explained the concept in lesson three, and after listening to him lecture for an hour, the idea of finding the area of quadrilaterals was as clear as mud for me.

2. Over the weekend, my grandpa had me and my brother paint his entire basement and remove his carpet. That was about as fun as plucking my eyebrows.

3. My science teacher has been working on experiments with boiling water all week long. This activity was about as exciting as going to the dentist and getting my teeth pulled.

PUNS

Underline the pun used in the following sentences. Then, explain why that is an example of a pun.

4. The glue salesman really stuck to his schedule and traveled to three cities in five days.

5. The principal was shocked to hear that a tree was struck by lighting on the playground.

6. Santa arrived at 11:59 on Christmas Eve. He came in the nick of time as little Joey woke up at 12:30 to see if there were any presents under the tree.

Week 10 Writing

Topic 2 Narrative Conclusions

Narratives are stories that focus on a character or characters. Narratives need to start with a catchy opening, be focused on the character and the setting, and have a strong plot that contains intriguing conflict. The narrative conclusion also needs to tie up loose ends and conclude the conflict.

Read the narrative below. Then, answer the questions that follow.

Tatum knew that something exciting was about to happen because his mother and father made him stay in the house.

"Mom, can I please get up now?" exclaimed Tatum.

"No, your father is not finished yet," said his mother from the kitchen.

Today was Tatum's birthday and he was so excited to see his gift. After sitting on the couch for what seemed to Tatum like five years, his dad finally called from the back yard.

"Okay, Tatum, come here!" shouted his father excitedly.

Tatum ran as fast as he could to the back yard. There he saw the most impressive swing set he has ever seen.

"Wow!" screamed Tatum, "This is the swing set from the magazine!"

As Tatum and his older sister Jill explored the swing set, their father left to go pick up their oldest sister from the library.

While Jill and Tatum played on the swings, the phone rang and Jill's mother could hear it from the porch outside.

Jill's mother said, "Be careful you two. I am going to go get the phone. I bet it's your grandmother." Jill's mother walked into the house to get the phone.

Meanwhile, Tatum was using his imagination and was acting like a robber running away from a crime. Tatum stood on the very top of the slide. He then grabbed the rope. Tatum jumped down the slide with the rope and the rope somehow slipped out of his hands. **TO BE CONTINUED...**

1. This narrative is missing a conclusion. Write a conclusion to this story.

....
....
....
....

Week 10 Science
Topic 1 Genotypes and Phenotypes

1. What are genes? ....

....

Genes are passed down from the mother and father to their offspring. These genes affect the offspring's traits. These traits are the offspring's appearance, behavior, and any diseases they may possess.

> Genes may have alleles.

2. What are alleles? ....

....

> They are often characterized as genotypes and phenotypes.

3. What are genotypes? ....

4. What are phenotypes? ....

When describing the genotype of an organism, it may have a combination of alleles. For instance, when referring to a puppy, it may have soft fur (SS), rough fur (ss), or a combination (Ss). The phenotype then is what is observable. So with the puppy, it either has soft fur or rough fur.

FITNESS PLANET → Let's get some fitness in! Go to page 167 to try some fitness activities.

Week 10 Science
Topic 1 Genotypes and Phenotypes

Let's practice!

5. A man named James is breeding parrots. Some of the baby parrots have green feathers and the other baby parrots have blue feathers. The gene for the color of the feathers have two alleles. The allele for green feathers is (F) and the allele for blue feathers is (f). James took out baby number six. He is labeled (ff). What color feathers does baby number six have? ....
....

6. Mrs. Sausa is going to a breeder for goldendoodles to get a puppy for her son's birthday. The breeder explained that there are puppies that are dark brown (B) and puppies that are light brown (b). The next day, Mrs. Sausa's son opened the box and there was a goldendoodle puppy (BB). What color is the puppy? ....
....

7. Aaron was looking forward to his two Hermit crabs, Lila and Edgar, having babies. He wondered if they were going to have gray shells (G) like Lila, or white shells (g) like Edgar. When they arrived, he got a baby hermit crab named Leo (GG), a baby hermit crab named Elray (gg), and a baby hermit crab named Gina (Gg). What did the three baby hermit crabs look like? ....
....

Week 10 Math
Topic 3 The Counting Principle

1. Jamie is making outfits for her doll that consist of 1 shirt and 1 skirt. Jamie has 6 shirts and 4 skirts for her doll. How many possible outfits can Jamie make?

2. An ice cream shop has 30 flavors, 25 different toppings and 3 types of cones. For $4 you can pick one type of cone, one flavor of ice cream and one topping. How many different combinations can you make for the $4 deal?

3. At a Mexican restaurant, you can make your own meal by choosing one option from each category below. How many different meals can customers create?

Taco Options	Chicken, Beef, Pork, Fish
Rice Options	Cilantro Rice, Mexican Rice
Bean Options	Pinto Beans, Refried Beans, Black Beans
Side Options	Salad, Coleslaw, Chips

4. A restaurant offers a lunch special where you choose 1 type of sandwich, 1 type of soup and 1 type of salad for $10. There are 5 choices of sandwiches, 3 choices of soups and 3 choices of salads. How many possible lunch combinations can you make?

5. A school is choosing one student from each grade to form a committee. There are 100 freshmen, 95 sophomores, 80 juniors and 82 seniors in the school. How many different committees could they form?

6. An ID number is made up of 1 letter from A to Z and 1 digit from 0 to 9. How many different ID numbers can be made.

Week 10 Math

Topic 4 Sample Space of Compound Events

1. You roll a 6-sided die and flip a coin. Make a tree diagram showing all possible outcomes.

2. You roll two 6-sided dice. How many possible outcomes are there?

3. A lunch shop offers the following choices for sandwich toppings. You must choose exactly one topping from each category. How many possible sandwiches can be made in this way?

Bread	Wheat, white
Meat	Turkey, Ham, Roast Beef
Vegetables	Tomato, Lettuce
Cheese	Cheddar, Swiss, Provolone

4. You spin the spinner below and choose a card out of a deck of 20 cards numbered 1-20. How many possible outcomes are there?

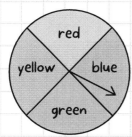

5. Finish filling in the tree diagram showing all possible outcomes if you flip 3 coins.

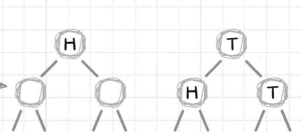

6. Jill is buying her friend a necklace as a birthday gift. She can choose a chain in gold, silver or white and a gem that is pink, turquoise, yellow, red or purple. How many different types of necklaces can Jill make?

Week 10 Reading
Topic 1 Author's Purpose

The author's purpose is why an author wrote about a particular topic and what it means to them. Read the passage below. Then, answer the questions that follow.

What is double the size of Texas and floats in the Pacific Ocean? That would be the Great Pacific Garbage Patch. According to pictures taken from airplanes, helicopters, and drones; the Great Pacific Garbage Patch includes over seventy thousand tons of plastic and other garbage remains. Currently, this patch floats between the states of California and Hawaii in the Pacific Ocean.

Where in the world does this plastic and trash come from? It comes from everyday trash that was misplaced. All of this trash eventually made its way into the ocean. One major issue that caused this plastic to drift to sea is that humans do not recycle cardboard and plastic like they should. This material then gets discarded inappropriately, and that material is then haphazardly tossed in the garbage. Then some of it, through poor discarding, finds itself in the serene ocean where it does not belong. Unfortunately, one great quality of plastic is that it does not disintegrate. This is a positive quality on land when using it, but a negative quality when it is residing in the ocean. Another reason why many environmentalists think the Great Pacific Garbage Patch has grown in recent years is due to the 2011 tsunami that hit Japan. It gathered garbage from the land and washed it out to sea.

Even though the Great Pacific Garbage Patch is the largest floating conglomerate of garbage, it sadly isn't the only one. Floating garbage keeps appearing all over the world. Many groups and organizations try and attempt to clean it up, but even after a whole day of work, they only get a meager percentage of what is there as it is too wide, heavy, and deep. So the next time you are throwing away a plastic bag from the grocery store, make sure that it doesn't end up in the Great Pacific Garbage Patch.

FITNESS PLANET → Let's get some fitness in! Go to page 167 to try some fitness activities.

Week 10　Writing
Topic 2　Writing a Narrative

1. What is the author's purpose for writing this passage?

   ....
   ....
   ....

2. What is their viewpoint regarding this topic?

   ....
   ....
   ....

3. Does the author appeal to pathos or the reader's emotions? Explain.

   ....
   ....
   ....

4. Does the author appeal to logos or the reader's logic? Explain.

   ....
   ....
   ....

5. What is the author's tone?

   ....
   ....
   ....

Week 10 Math

Topic 5 Probabilities of Compound Events

1. You roll a 6-sided die and flip a coin. What is the probability of rolling a 5 and the coin landing heads up?

2. You flip 3 coins. What is the probability of at least two of them landing tails up?

3. You roll a 6-sided die and flip a coin. What is the probability of rolling an odd number and the coin landing tails up?

4. You spin a spinner and toss a coin. What is the probability of spinning a red and the coin landing heads up?

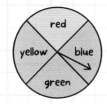

5. You spin a spinner and roll a 6-sided die. What is the probability of spinning a green or yellow and the coin landing tails up?

6. A lunch shop offers the following choices for sandwich toppings. You must choose exactly one topping from each category. What is the probability of randomly choosing a turkey sandwich with tomato and provolone on wheat bread?

Bread	Wheat, white
Meat	Turkey, Ham, Roast Beef
Vegetables	Tomato, Lettuce
Cheese	Cheddar, Swiss, Provolone

Week 10 Social Studies
Topic 1 The Middle East

> Let's learn about the Middle East! If you need help with some of these questions, ask an adult or use the Internet to learn about the Middle East.

1. The Middle East is made up of many countries. These countries reside in two continents. Name them.

    a. ....

    b. ....

2. The Middle East is touching many bodies of water. Name them.

    a. ....

    b. ....

    c. ....

    d. ....

    e. ....

    f. ....

3. The Middle East has three important rivers that run through it. Name them.

    a. ....

    b. ....

    c. ....

4. What are the two most important natural resources from the Middle East? Name them.

    a. ....

    b. ....

5. Research The Middle East and discover five facts about the region.

    a. ....

    b. ....

    c. ....

    d. ....

    e. ....

Grade 7-8
WEEK 11

Get ready to learn about:

- synonyms and antonyms
- punnett squares
- dialogue
- The Reconstruction Era and more!

Week 11 Math
Topic 1 Review Week 1

1. Daniel walks $\frac{3}{5}$ mile in $\frac{1}{2}$ hour. At this rate, how far will he walk in 1.5 hours?

2. What is the constant of proportionality in the equation $y = 12x$?

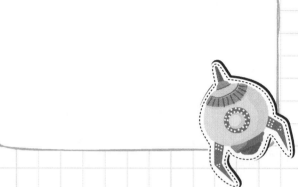

3. Does the following table show a proportional relationship between x and y?

x	4	4.5	5
y	10	9	8

4. Adam spent $15 on 2 video games. The equation $y = 7.5x$ represents this situation where x is the number of video games and y is the total cost. What does 7.5 mean in this situation?

5. A clothing store has a markup rate of 75%. The new jackets that just arrived cost $28 wholesale. What is the retail price after the markup?

6. What is the constant of proportionality between y and x?

x	5	10	15
y	2	4	6

Week 11 Math
Topic 2 Review Week 2

1. The ratio 60:9 is equivalent to ___ :6?

2. The table shows a proportional relationship between c and d. Write an equation that describes the relationship between c and d.

c	d
17.5	35
2.75	5.5
14	28

3. Use the graph to write an equation that describes the relationship between x and y.

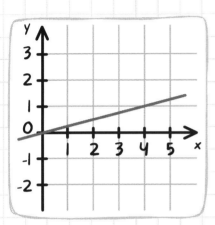

4. Which line has a constant of proportionality between y and x of 1?

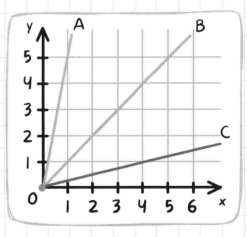

5. Lisa, Kevin and Paul share a pizza and ice cream at a restaurant. The total before tax is $35.08. The tax rate is 8.5% and they will tip 15% after tax. They will divide the total in thirds so they each pay an equal amount. How much will each person owe?

6. Lucas types at a constant rate. He needs 15 minutes to type a total of 500 words. Write an equation that describes the relationship between t, the time, and w, the number of words typed.

FITNESS PLANET → Let's get some fitness in! Go to page 167 to try some fitness activities.

143

Week 11 Language
Topic 1 Antonyms and Synonyms

1. What are synonyms?
   ....
2. What are antonyms?
   ....

Synonyms

In the following sentences, look at the bolded word. Write a synonym that fits in the sentence. Remember, a word may be a synonym but it might not fit in the context of the sentence.

1. Janice decorated her Christmas tree with **opulent** ornaments she gathered from her many adventures around the world. ....

2. Mr. Gen was **suspicious** that Taryn and Leo cheated on the math final, but he had no proof. ....

3. Eric is a musical **prodigy**. She is only seven, but she can play eight instruments. She also writes her own music and has appeared as a featured soloist at many symphonic concerts. ....

4. William is an **adept** woodworker. He has crafted many shelves and grandfather clocks. ....

Antonyms

For the following sentences, find the antonym of the bolded word. Then, using the information and characters in the previous sentences, rewrite the sentences to fit the altered word.

5. Antonym of opulent - ....
6. Sentence - ....
7. Antonym of suspicious - ....
8. Sentence - ....
9. Antonym of prodigy - ....
10. Sentence - ....
11. Antonym of adept - ....
12. Sentence - ....

Week 11   Reading
Topic 2   Dialogue

What is dialogue?

Dialogue is when a character talks aloud in a story. This is indicated by quotation marks. Dialogue helps the audience understand who the character is by what the characters say, what they don't say, and what others say about them.

Read the passage that contains dialogue below. Then, answer the questions that follow.

"Sit down, now!" said Jake's father. He was ready to finally talk to his son after the big explosion the night before. "Now listen, son. I know that I was quite angry yesterday when you mentioned that you didn't want to go to college next year. I am sorry I got so angry. I have calmed down now, but I must tell you. You are making a big mistake."

"It's not a mistake dad," noted Jake who was frustrated with this father for not listening to him.

"You will be wasting your life if you don't go to college!" exclaimed Jake's father.

"That is absolutely ridiculous. Lots of people have become successful without a college degree, like Steve Jobs for instance" mentioned Jake.

"That is rare, extremely rare. Look, son, I didn't go to college. I couldn't. I had to go and make money for my young family. I had to work in a hot and dirty factory and I didn't earn much money. I regret not going to college and I don't want you to regret it!"

1. What does the dialogue reveal about Jake?

   ....

   ....

2. What does the dialogue reveal about Jake's father?

   ....

   ....

3. Was using dialogue the best way for the author to reveal the characterization of Jake and Jake's father? Explain.

   ....

   ....

   ....

Week 11 Science
Topic 1 Punnett Squares

You learned about genes and alleles in the previous lesson, now let's put them in punnett squares to see the choices of the offspring.

To demonstrate, let's go back to the story about the parrots. Some of the parrots had green feathers (F) and some parrots had blue feathers (f). What are the possible results of an offspring? The results are shown in the punnett square blow.

Circle the parrot with all blue feathers.

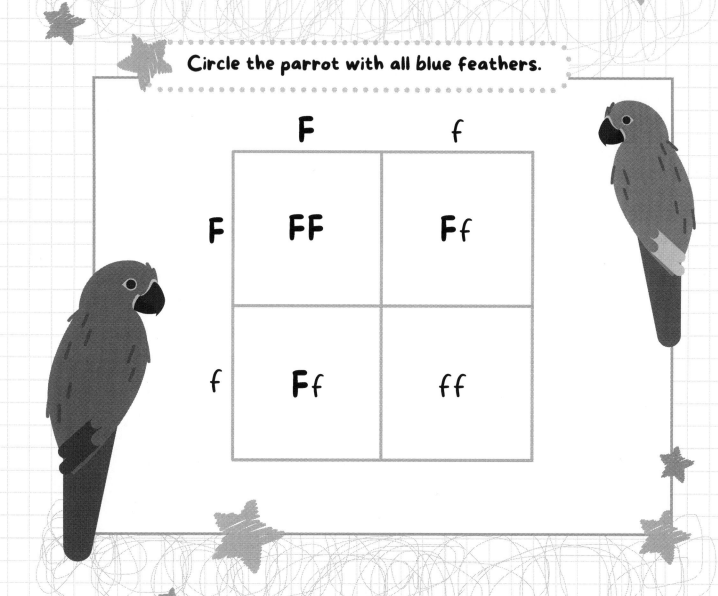

146

Week 11 — Science
Topic 1 — Punnett Squares

Now complete punnett squares for the next two scenarios.

1. Mrs. Sausa is going to a breeder for goldendoodles to get a puppy for her son's birthday. The breeder explained that there are puppies that are dark brown (B) and puppies that are light brown (b). The next day, Mrs. Sausa's son opened the box and there was a goldendoodle puppy (BB). Fill in the punnett square. Then, circle the characteristics of Mrs. Sausa's son's new puppy.

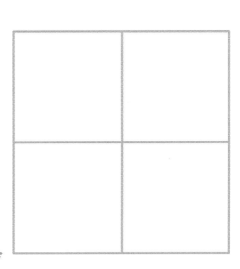

2. Aaron was looking forward to his two Hermit crabs, Lila and Edgar, having babies. He wondered if they were going to have gray shells (G) like Lila, or white shells (g) like Edgar. When they arrived, he got a baby hermit crab named Leo (GG), a baby hermit crab named Elray (gg), and a baby hermit crab named Gina (Gg). Fill in the punnett square. Then, circle and label the characteristics for the three crabs.

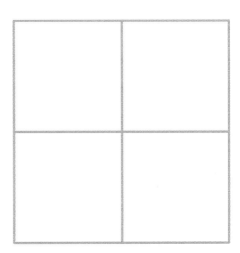

FITNESS PLANET → Let's get some fitness in! Go to page 167 to try some fitness activities.

Week 11   Math

Topic 3   Review Week 3

1. Is $f + (-g)$ negative or positive?

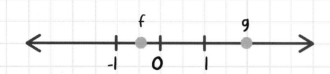

2. Use the number line to find the missing value: $-4 - \underline{} = -7$

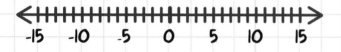

3. $3.5 \div -1.4$

4. $5\frac{2}{3} - 1\frac{1}{4} + \frac{1}{6}$

5. Simplify $\dfrac{4\frac{4}{7}}{1\frac{6}{7}}$

6. $-\dfrac{8}{5} \div 1.4$

Week 11 Math
Topic 4 Review Week 4

1. Rewrite 1.65 as a reduced fraction.

2. Rewrite $1\frac{4}{15}$ as a decimal.

3. $-7 + (-14) - 2$

4. $-12 \times (-11)$

5. Put the following numbers in order from least to greatest: 9.1, $9\frac{1}{8}$, 9.02

6. Sam's making pecan pies for the holidays, so he buys 4.25 pounds of pecans in the bulk section of the grocery store. The pecans cost $9 per pound. How much did Sam spend?

Week 11 Reading
Topic 3 Evaluating An Argument

Read the nonfiction argumentative passage below. Then, answer the questions that follow.

While many think that animal testing is cruel and insensitive, there are many positive reasons for animal testing and thus, this process of using animals for medical testing should continue. First, testing on animals, specifically for medical purposes, has helped countless individuals. For example, testing on dogs has led to the discovery and implementation of insulin, which is used for patients suffering from diabetes. The polio vaccine was also tested on animals, and then given to humans to stop dangerous outbreaks. Animal testing has also helped find cures or medicines for cancer, leukemia, maleria, cystic fibrosis, and tuberculosis, just to name a few.

Secondly, animals and humans have similar body systems which explains why scientists conduct medical tests on animals. Many animals have similar nervous systems, endocrine systems, and immune systems to humans. This makes testing easier so scientists can compare their structures to those of humans and can see positive and similar results. Chimpanzees and mice have very similar DNA to animals, as well as common organ types, which is why these animals are usually test subjects. .

Lastly, while harming animals is not ideal, testing on animals eliminates the deaths of humans. If there was no prior testing, many humans could die when taking new medications or enduring new procedures. This testing is not done haphazardly, but with great care and diligence. There are many rules and laws that protect these animals. They have to be housed in spacious cages with the right temperature, and have access to clean food and water. They also have to be tested and visited by veterinarians.

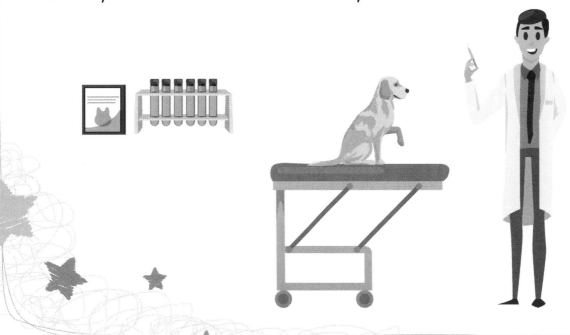

Week 11 Reading

Topic 3 Evaluating An Argument

1. How many points or reasons does the author of this passage give for why animal testing should be implemented?

   ....

2. What is the first reason why testing should be implemented? Do you agree or disagree with this reason? Explain.

   ....

   ....

3. What is one counterargument you can use to go against the author's first point?

   ....

4. What is the second reason why testing should be implemented? Do you agree or disagree with this reason? Explain.

   ....

   ....

5. What is one counterargument you can use to go against the author's second point?

   ....

6. What is the third reason why testing should be implemented? Do you agree or disagree with this reason? Explain.

   ....

   ....

7. What is one counterargument you can use to go against the author's third point?

   ....

 FITNESS PLANET  Let's get some fitness in! Go to page 167 to try some fitness activities.

Week 11 Math
Topic 5 Review Week 5

1. Simplify: $(4x^2 + 3x) - (2x - x^2 + 7)$

2. Expand and simplify: $-5a(2a + 4) - a^2$

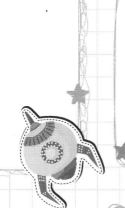

3. Are the expressions $3a + 3$ and $3(a + 3)$ equivalent?

4. Rewrite in the form a^b: $a^3 a^7$

5. Rewrite in the form x^n: $\dfrac{x^7}{x^2}$

6. Solve $15 \leq a - 8$

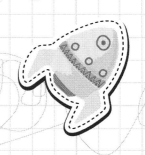

Week 11 Social Studies

Topic 1 The Reconstruction Era

Read the paragraph below, and fill in the missing words.

During the time of the Civil War, the .... (South, North) wanted to be separated from the United States. Their plan was to have a country called the .... (Confederate, United) States of America. However, after .... (two, four) years of fighting in a cruel and bloody war, it finally ended and the South .... (won, lost) the war. This meant that .... (slavery, sharecropping) ended. However, just because they were .... (free, enslaved) at the end of the war didn't mean too much since the former slaves did not have money or means of finding a job.

The time after the war ended was called the .... (Reconstruction, New World) Era. The Republicans at that time wanted to reconstruct or .... (change, demolish) the South. They wanted to .... (replace, leave) the current leaders, construct more .... (stores, schools) so African Americans could learn, build and construct .... (roads, railroads) for trade, and lower .... (taxes, funds) on businesses. To go against these changes, many Caucasian Democrats created violent groups like the .... (Ku Klux Klan, Freedom Riders) and there was a lot of hatred towards the .... (African Americans / Caucasians).

In 1866, an important change occurred in the Reconstruction Era. A law passed in .... (Congress, the Senate) which gave that African Americans rights to write up .... (contracts, land deeds). This allowed African Americans to get .... (control, power) over what was theirs. This allowed African Americans to buy and own items, to work, own land, and to get married.

153

Grade 7-8
WEEK 12

Now let's finish up with:

- connotation and denotation
- editing
- cellular respiration
- conflicting information and more!

Week 12   Math
Topic 1   Review Week 6

1. Solve for k: $4k = k - 20$

2. Solve for f: $10 = 2f - 16$

3. A greenhouse has a length that is three times its width. The perimeter of the greenhouse is 72 feet. Write an equation that can be used to find the length and width. Then solve the equation to find the dimensions of the greenhouse.

4. Solve for y: $0.3 = 4y + 9.9$

5. Solve for a: $7a < a + 3$

6. The soccer team is doing a fundraiser where they're selling car washes. They spent $60 on supplies and are charging $8 for each car wash. Write an inequality you could solve to find how many car washes they need to sell to earn at least $500.

Week 12 Math
Topic 2 Review Week 7

1. A scale on a travel map shows that 0.5 inch represents 30 miles. What number of inches on the map represent 105 actual miles?

2. Draw a scaled copy of rectangle X with a scale factor of 0.5.

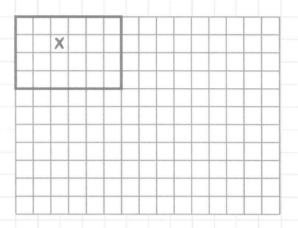

3. Square LMNO has side lengths 2.5 ft. Square WXYZ has side lengths 15 ft. What is the scale factor from square WXYZ to square LMNO?

4. Could 1, 1, and 2 be the side lengths of a triangle?

5. Find the missing side of the right triangle.

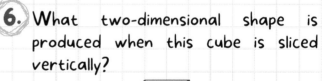

6. What two-dimensional shape is produced when this cube is sliced vertically?

FITNESS PLANET → Let's get some fitness in! Go to page 167 to try some fitness activities.

Week 12 Language

Topic 1 Connotation and Denotation

1. What is a connotation?
   ....

2. What is a denotation?
   ....

Many times, in speaking and writing, society has instilled many connotations into our writing, rather than just using denotations. This is not a bad thing, as connotations add detail and insight; however, some connotations may be negative in certain situations or settings.

Read the sentences below. Then, identify whether the bolded word has a denotative definition, a positive connotative definition, or a negative connotative definition.

3. Gerald was in trouble for **defacing** the public library. ....

4. My teacher is so **conservative**. She feels like we should live like children in the 1800s and not talk. ....

5. My grandmother was a **glut** of Star Wars. She had every figurine and poster possible. ....

6. The class was **serene** after the teacher announced that the test was cancelled. ....

7. Michael **mustered** up enough courage to tell his teacher about what was in Ellen's backpack. ....

8. That party was so **lit** that I was disappointed that I had to leave when that my mom picked me up at 9:30. ....

Week 12　Writing

Topic 1　Editing Practice

After you are finished with a writing assignment, you are not done! Is important to make sure that the structure, organization, and content of your essay aligns with the directions your teacher gave you. Also, you need to make sure you edit your work to eliminate run-on sentences, fragments, and capitalization / punctuation errors. The editing stage is also the perfect time to strengthen your word choice and exchange common words for stronger synonyms.

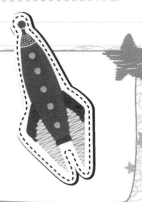

Read the passage below. Then, edit it and write the corrected paragraph under it.

Adults and Teenagers a like have there cellphones close-at-hand and frequently look at them whenever they can. Kids take there cellphones with wher ever they go to, but should they students bring there cellphones to school with them.

It is fact that many student own cell phones and those numbers continue to climb in recent years as students get there first cell phones at a young ages and children as young as fourth fifth grade can be seen with a cell phone in their hand and they bring their cellphones to the school.

Their has been a lot many. This Controversy surrounded whether or not cell phones should be aloud in schools and the consensus has yet to be decided regarded this issue depending on individual school systems they will decide if students can bring phones to school.

many school officials donot want cell phones brought into schools because they'll feel it will be a major distraction. They'll feel that students will be focused on social media and texting their friends than more focused on the subjects they are learning. Many high schools and middle schools have made a rule that cell phones are to be put away in their students pockets or bookbags during class other the other hand teachers like this type of technology and use it the use of cellphones into what they are learned in class.

Other rules that have been implemented regarding cell phones use includes students using their phones only during the recess, passing periods, and lunches. However many disagree with there students using their phones during lunch because they feel that this lessons interaction with other students. They fear that students will lose face-to-face conversations if they have their phones to focus on during this time. With fear that cell phones will become a distractions, why do parents want their child to bring a cell phone to school? The major reason is safety and parents want their children to have a phone in case of an emergency.

Week 12 Science
Topic 1 Cellular Respiration

Cellular respiration occurs within cells to convert or change food into energy. This is how we get our energy to run a 5k or work out in the mornings. Cellular respiration occurs due to many chemical reactions and breaks down the food we eat in order to use fuel our bodies.

The equation for cellular respiration is:

Glucose + Oxygen - produces - Carbon Dioxide + Water

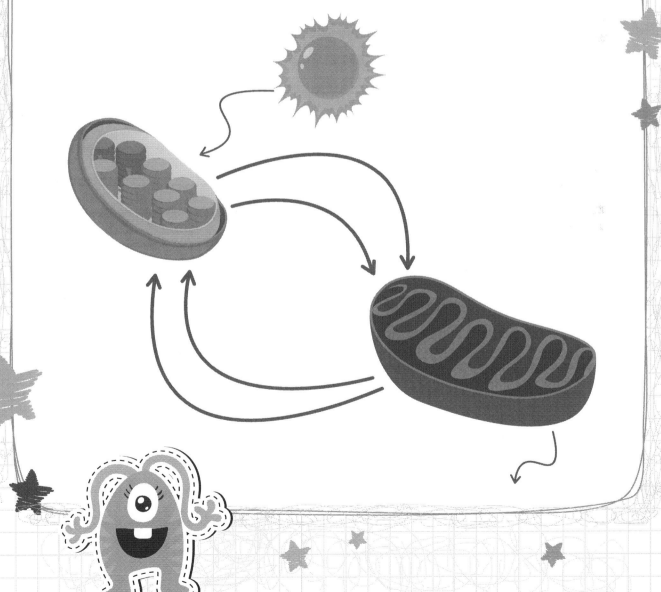

Week 12 — Science
Topic 1 — Cellular Respiration

1. What serves as an energy source for cells?

   ....
   ....

2. What is glucose?

   ....
   ....

3. What are the products in the equation above?

   ....
   ....

4. What are the reactants in the equation above?

   ....
   ....

5. In your own words, describe the process of cellular respiration.

   ....
   ....
   ....
   ....
   ....
   ....
   ....
   ....

Week 12　Math
Topic 3　Review Week 8

1. Find the complement of 54°.

2. Find the supplement of 79°.

3. Find the area of a circle with diameter 18 meters.

4. Find the circumference of a circle with radius 15 cm.

5. What are the coordinates of point P(-1, 2) after a translation of 3 units left and 2 units up?

6. Triangle ABC has an area of 5 square cm. After a rotation of 90°, how has the area of triangle ABC changed?

   A. The area has increased.
   B. The area has decreased.
   C. The area remains unchanged.

FITNESS PLANET → Let's get some fitness in! Go to page 167 to try some fitness activities.

Week 12 Math
Topic 4 Review Week 9

1. On the multiple choice section of a standardized test, there are four answer choices that are equally likely to be used on each question (A, B, C, D). On question 10, what is the probability that the answer is D?

2. You flipped a coin 100 times and it landed heads up 39 times and tails up 61 times. What is the probability the coin will land heads up the next time you flip it?

3. A deck of cards contains 20 blue cards, 40 red cards, 15 yellow cards and 25 green cards. What is the probability of randomly choosing a blue card from the deck?

4. The city randomly sampled some of its population asking where they prefer to grocery shop. Here are the results:

Store	Number
Fresh Market	18
Henry's	35
GT's Grocery	12
Proctor's	5

Based on the results, how many of the city's 50,000 residents prefer to shop at Henry's?

5. The histograms show the number of money spent eating out by participants in a study on budgeting. What piece of information can be gathered from these histograms?

A. The participants in group 1 spent more on eating out on average.

B. The participants in group 2 spent more on eating out on average.

C. None of the above.

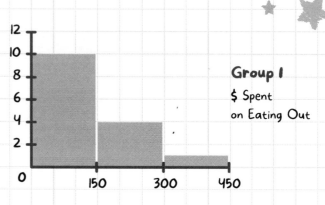

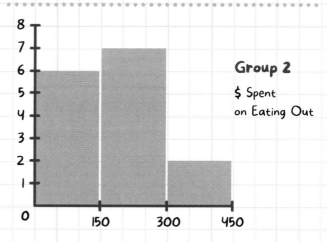

6. The Gimble family has a movie night every Friday night. They are trying to decide what movie to watch. They own 8 cartoons, 5 comedies, 2 documentaries, and 4 dramas. They randomly pick one movie to watch. What is the probability they randomly choose a comedy?

Week 12   Reading
Topic 3   Conflicting Information

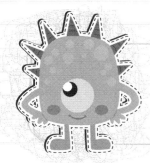

Sometimes texts conflict with each other and you have to decide what information is accurate and what information to believe.

Below are two passages on the same topic, but they argue against each other. Read the passages and then complete the questions that follow.

Passage One

Some individuals may feel that medical animal testing is positive as it is used to find medicines and vaccines that cure humans; however, they are wrong because animal testing is inhumane and should be against the law. First, animal testing, even doing it medically, is cruel, harsh, and should not be allowed. Animals are not treated well by scientists during the testing process. They are often starved and not feed properly. To test certain medicines, scientists often have to injure an animal. They are often burned, cut, or have one of their bones broken. Thousands and thousands of animals are killed each and every year due to medical testing and this is wrong because these tests should be completed in a different manner.

Next, scientists should not be using animals for medical testing as it is cruel, and instead, they should be using different methods. For example, scientists can test human cells. This would be accurate and not hurt a human being or an animal. This can be taken out of humans in a simple blood test, and if it doesn't work, then no animal or human is harmed. Different fake organs are also being developed to mimic real organs. Those should be used instead of animals because again, if something goes wrong, no animal or human is harmed.

Lastly, animals shouldn't be used in medical tests as those tests are not accurate because animals are different from humans. The makeup of animals are vastly different than humans, especially the weight difference. The results of the tests are not accurate and should not be used anyway as it may cause harm to humans. For example, a study was completed on pregnant mice to see if a sleeping drug would affect the mother. In the study, it did not show any side effects; however, when given to humans, the unborn child was affected. This shows that animal tests are not always accurate.

Week 12 Reading

Topic 3 Conflicting Information

Passage Two

While many think that animal testing is cruel and insensitive, there are many positive reasons for animal testing and thus, this process of using animals for medical testing should continue. First, testing on animals, specifically for medical purposes, has helped countless individuals. For example, testing on dogs has led to the discovery and implementation of insulin, which is used for patients suffering from diabetes. The polio vaccine was also tested on animals, and then given to humans to stop dangerous outbreaks. Animal testing has also helped find cures or medicines for cancer, leukemia, malaria, cystic fibrosis, and tuberculosis, just to name a few.

Secondly, animals and humans have similar body systems which explains why scientists conduct medical tests on animals. Many animals have similar nervous systems, endocrine systems, and immune systems to humans. This makes testing easier so scientists can compare their structures to those of humans and can see positive and similar results. Chimpanzees and mice have very similar DNA to animals, as well as common organ types, which is why these animals are usually test subjects.

Lastly, while harming animals is not ideal, testing on animals eliminates the deaths of humans. If there was no prior testing, many humans could die when taking new medications or enduring new procedures. This testing is not done haphazardly, but with great care and diligence. There are many rules and laws that protect these animals. They have to be housed in spacious cages with the right temperature, and have access to clean food and water. They also have to be tested and visited by veterinarians.

1. What is one idea that the two passages conflict on?

   a. What does text one believe? ....

   b. What does text two believe? ....

2. Which one do you feel is more persuasive? Explain.

   ....

3. What is another idea that the two passages conflict on?

   a. What does text one believe? ....

   b. What does text two believe? ....

4. Which one do you feel is more persuasive? Explain.

   ....

   ....

Week 12 Math
Topic 5 Review Week 10

1. If the probability of an event is 1, circle which of the following is true:

   A. The event will happen.
   B. The event will not happen.
   C. There is an equally likely chance the event will or will not happen.

2. True or False: An event cannot have a probability of 0.

3. Find the probability of randomly choosing a white marble out of a bag containing 10 white, 2 black, 6 blue, 18 green and 11 yellow marbles.

4. Tim wears sneakers, pants, a t-shirt and a hat every day. He has 3 pairs of sneakers, 4 pairs of pants, 7 t-shirts and 2 hats. How many different outfits can he make?

5. Find the probability of rolling a 6-sided die twice and getting a 1 both times.

6. Find the probability of tossing a coin 4 times and having it land tails up every time.

Week 12 Social Studies

Topic 1 The Beginning of the Civil War

1. What is a civil war?
   ....

2. Why do you think a civil war is sometimes more emotional and upsetting than a foreign war? Explain.
   ....

3. Who was fighting in the American Civil War?

   a. The Union who was from the .... (North, South)

   b. The Confederacy from the .... (North, South)

4. In the election right before the war, who was elected president? ....

5. This made the South nervous as they didn't want what to end? ....

6. Which side decided to succeed and break off from the United States? ....

7. In your opinion, why was the American Civil War started?
   ....

 FITNESS PLANET → Let's get some fitness in! Go to page 167 to try some fitness activities.

FITNESS PLANET

Grade 7-8

FITNESS PLANET
Repeat these exercises 2 ROUNDS

exercises complex one

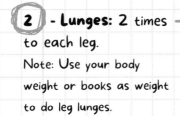

② - **Lunges:** 2 times to each leg.
Note: Use your body weight or books as weight to do leg lunges.

① - **Abs:** 3 times

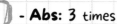

③ - **Plank:** 6 sec.

④ - **Run:** 50m
Note: Run 25 meters to one side and 25 meters back to the starting position.

Please be aware of your environment and be safe at all times. If you cannot do an exercise, just try your best.

exercises complex two

① - **High Plank:** 6 sec.

③ - **Waist Hooping:** 10 times.
Note: if you do not have a hoop, pretend you have an imaginary hoop and rotate your hips 10 times.

② - **Chair:** 10 sec.
Note: sit on an imaginary chair, keep your back straight.

④ - **Abs:** 10 times

FITNESS PLANET
Repeat these exercises 2 ROUNDS

exercises complex three

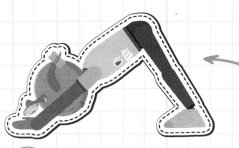

1 - **Down Dog:** 10 sec.

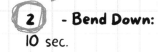

2 - **Bend Down:** 10 sec.

3 - **Chair:** 10 sec.

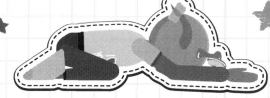

4 - **Child Pose:** 20 sec.

5 - **Shavasana:** as long as you can. Note: think of happy moments and relax your mind.

 Please be aware of your environment and be safe at all times. If you cannot do an exercise, just try your best.

exercises complex four

2 - **Lunges:** 3 times to each leg.
Note: Use your body weight or books as weight to do leg lunges.

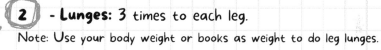

4 - **Abs:** 10 times

1 - **Bend forward:** 10 times.
Note: try to touch your feet. Make sure to keep your back straight and if needed you can bend your knees.

3 - **Plank:** 6 sec.

169

ANSWER SHEET

Week 1

★ Week 1 ★ Math

★ Topic 1 ★ Ratios

★ Page 12 ★

1. $\dfrac{2}{3}$
2. $\dfrac{11}{16}$
3. $\dfrac{16}{5}$ or $3\dfrac{1}{5}$ mile
4. $\dfrac{8}{21}$
5. $\dfrac{27}{28}$
6. $\dfrac{33}{40}$

★ Topic 2 ★ Constant of Proportionality (Unit Rate)

★ Page 13 ★

1. 6
2. $\dfrac{1}{3}$
3. $\dfrac{1}{3}$
4. 4
5. 2
6. 6

★ Topic 3 ★ Recognizing Proportional Relationships

★ Page 18 ★

1. Yes
2. No
3. 6
4. Yes
5. No
6. No

★ Topic 4 ★ Comparing and Interpreting Constants of Proportionality

★ Page 19 ★

1. b
2. Mark drove 55 miles per hour.
3. A
4. Each avocado costs $1.50.
5. Grace

★ Topic 5 ★ Discount and Markup Problems

★ Page 22 ★

1. $39.20
2. $260
3. $16.83
4. $140
5. $20.80
6. $840

171

ANSWER SHEET

★ Week 1 ★ Reading
★ Topic 1 ★ Compare and Contrast Structures
★ Page 15 ★

Answers may vary.
1. I think this is event structure because Mrs. Darling seeks to figure out who Peter is.
2. This shows that Peter will be an important figure in the story.
3. This is character structure because it shows what Mrs. Lynde believes, thinks, and feels.
4. This gives insight into Mrs. Lynde and how nosey she really is.
5. Both of these structures involve a character trying to solve something. Mrs. Darling wants to know who Peter is, and Mrs. Lynde wants to know where Matthew is going.
6. Passage two focuses more on the characterization of Mrs. Lynde and her trying to figure out where Matthew is going.

★ Week 1 ★ Language Review
★ Topic 2 ★ Verbals
★ Page 20 ★

1. I
2. G
3. P
4. I
5. G
6. P
7. G
8. P

★ Week 1 ★ Reading
★ Topic 3 ★ Context Clues and Vocabulary
★ Page 21 ★

1. flashy
2. fight or struggle
3. opinion or suspicion
4. cruel and insensitive
5. exemption
6. important person

★ Week 1 ★ Science
★ Topic 1 ★ The Scientific Method
★ Page 16 ★

1. Figuring out what you want to find out
2. Identifying a question that you want answered
3. Experiment with the question
4. Record the findings
5. Use the findings to answer the question
6. Tell others what you have found and decided

ANSWER SHEET

★ **Topic 2** ★ **Identifying Terms**

★ **Page 17** ★

1. The group that receives the treatment
2. The group that doesn't receive the treatment
3. Control Group
4. Experimental Group
5. The variable that is changed
6. The variable that is not changed

★ **Week 1** ★ **Social Studies**

★ **Topic 1** ★ **The Bill of Rights**

★ **Page 23** ★

1st Amendment: The government cannot make everyone participate in the same religion.
2nd Amendment: The government cannot tell people they cannot have guns.
3rd Amendment: Soldiers cannot stay at someone's house without permission.
4th Amendment: Police officers cannot search someone's house without a warrant.
5th Amendment: Protects people from incriminating themselves
6th Amendment: Everyone has a right to a trial no matter who they are and what they did
7th Amendment: A jury is allowed to hear a case and decide, rather than just the judge.
8th Amendment: Protects people from paying heavy fines and bails.
9th Amendment: There are other rights of citizens that should be taken into account.
10th Amendment: States can have their own rules.

ANSWER SHEET

Week 2

★ Week 2 ★ Math

★ Topic 1 ★ Test for Equivalent Ratios

★ Page 25 ★

1. 48
2. 27
3. False
4. True
5. 10 inches
6. John

★ Topic 2 ★ Proportional Relationships as Equations

★ Page 26 ★

1. $r = \frac{2}{3}b$
2. $t = \frac{15}{20}a$ or $t = \frac{3}{4}a$
3. $c = 9.5t$
4. $d = 1.5c$
5. 93; The train travels at 93 miles per hour.

★ Topic 3 ★ Constant of Proportionality from Graphs

★ Page 31 ★

1. $\frac{1}{7}$
2. $\frac{1}{3}$
3. 2.5
4. 0.8 or $\frac{4}{5}$
5. $y = \frac{1}{2}x$

★ Topic 4 ★ Graphs of Proportional Relationships

★ Page 32 ★

1. $\frac{\$24}{hour}$
2. $\frac{1}{6}$
3. 7
4. 1.5 or $\frac{3}{2}$
5. A

★ Topic 5 ★ Percent Problems

★ Page 35 ★

1. $1728
2. $5.01
3. $15.11
4. $21.02
5. $1967.92
6. $117.83

ANSWER SHEET

★ Week 2 ★ Reading
★ Topic 1 ★ Character Development in Nonfiction

★ Page 28 ★

Answers may vary.
1. Jaime is goal driven. She had this idea after watching this occur on "her favorite Disney show growing up." She is also creative because she made many lemon flavored treats like "lemon sprinkle cookies, sugar lemon brownies, lemon cake pops, lemon cheesecake, and old fashioned lemon drop cookies."
2. Many of her customers thought this idea was superb and Jaime had a great business idea. Jaime "sold out of lemonade and all of her lemon flavored treats" showing that everyone liked her products. They also wanted her for many "different events and parties."
3. Jaime is creative due to her lemon flavored treats like "lemon cake pops," and she is also business minded to create lists and "budget."
4. Jaime possesses many business skills like "budgeting" and inventing and "concocting new items."
5. I think Jaime will major in business in college.

★ Week 2 ★ Language
★ Topic 2 ★ Active and Passive Voice

★ Page 33 ★

1. Active
2. Passive
3. Active
4. Passive
5. Active
6. Passive

Answers may vary.
7. I ate three platefuls of watermelon at the summer party.
8. The watermelon was devoured by Katie at the summer party.

175

ANSWER SHEET

★ Week 2 ★ Writing

★ Topic 3 ★ Expressing Your Opinion

★ Page 34 ★

Answers may vary.
1. a. Recycling
   b. Climate Change
   c. Starting School Later
   d. Issues in Hong Kong
   e. Buy Food Locally
2. Recycling
3. Plastic is ending up in the oceans and in landfills. People are not recycling like they should. Recycling should be mandatory.
4. a. Plastic is found in oceans.
   b. Plastic does not break down like other products in the landfill.
   c. Plastic products will eventually be cheaper.

★ Week 2 ★ Science

★ Topic 1 ★ Experimental Protocol

★ Page 29 ★	★ Page 30 ★
Answers vary	1. The experimental protocol includes the steps and materials needed in an experiment. 2. To spread through water 3. The dye diffuses into the water. 4. The color diffuses faster in the warm glass. 5. I learned that hotter water makes the dye diffuse faster.

★ Week 2 ★ Social Studies

★ Topic 1 ★ Italian Renaissance: Achievements in Art and Literature

★ Page 36 ★

1. Revival of art and literature
2. a. Michelangelo
   b. Raphael
   c. Donatello
3. Importance and focus on humans
4. a. *Hamlet* by William Shakespeare
   b. *Don Quixote* by Miguel de Cervantes Saavedra
   c. *Doctor Faustus* by Christopher Marlowe

ANSWER SHEET

Week 3

★ Week 3 ★ Math

★ Topic 1 ★ Add and Subtract Rational Numbers

★ Page 38 ★

1. 9.04
2. $\dfrac{95}{12}$
3. $-\dfrac{58}{35}$
4. -3.29
5. $\dfrac{7}{6}$
6. $\dfrac{13}{12}$

★ Topic 2 ★ Multiply and Divide Rational Numbers

★ Page 39 ★

1. $\dfrac{16}{91}$
2. $-22\dfrac{1}{6}$
3. -3.3605
4. -1.35
5. $2\dfrac{2}{7}$
6. $-\dfrac{5}{14}$

★ Topic 3 ★ Find the Missing Value

★ Page 44 ★

1. 8
2. -2
3. 8
4. -5
5. -15
6. -4

★ Topic 4 ★ Simplify Complex Fractions

★ Page 45 ★

1. $\dfrac{2}{3}$
2. $\dfrac{9}{5}$
3. $\dfrac{21}{8}$
4. $\dfrac{11}{26}$
5. 32
6. $-\dfrac{27}{38}$

★ Topic 5 ★ Number Line Operations

★ Page 48 ★

1. -3 - 5
2. -8 + 4
3. negative
4. positive
5. positive
6. negative

ANSWER SHEET

★ Week 3 ★ Reading
★ Topic 1 ★ Points of View

★ Page 41 ★

1. Third Person Objective
   The passage uses the keywords, he and her, as well as refers to a character's actions but not their thoughts.
2. Third Person Omniscient
   The narrator gets into the thoughts of both characters.
3. First Person
   It uses the keyword I. The person telling the story is Aria.

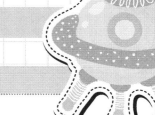

★ Week 3 ★ Language
★ Topic 2 ★ Moods

★ Page 46 ★

1. Indicative
2. Imperative
3. Subjunctive
4. Conditional
5. Interrogative
6. Indicative
7. Imperative
8. Subjunctive
9. Conditional
10. Interrogative

★ Week 3 ★ Writing
★ Topic 3 ★ Informative Writing

★ Page 47 ★

Answers will vary.
1. The country of Madagascar
2. a. https://www.britannica.com/place/Madagascar
   b. https://www.bbc.com/news/world-africa-13861843
   c. https://www.telegraph.co.uk/travel/destinations/africa/madagascar/articles/facts-about-madagascar/
3. a. Madagascar is an island. In fact it is the world's fourth largest island.
   b. Madagascar was discovered in **500AD**
   c. Madagascar has animals and insects that can only be seen there like the aye-aye lemur.
   d. There are not many train tracks in Madagascar.
   e. The national sport of Madagascar is fighting without gloves.

ANSWER SHEET

★ Week 3 ★ Science

★ Topic 1 ★ Density, Mass, and Volume

★ Page 42 ★

1. The degree of consistency
2. The quality of matter; the weight
3. The amount of space something occupies
4. .78
5. 5
6. 17.5

★ Topic 2 ★ Atoms and Chemical Elements

★ Page 43 ★

1. Basic unit of chemistry
2. The nucleus
3. Protons and neutrons.
4. A particle with a negative charge; travels around the nucleus.
5.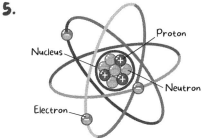

★ Week 3 ★ Social Studies

★ Topic 1 ★ The Louisiana Purchase

★ Page 49 ★

Answers may vary but there should be some rationales provided. Example: Jefferson probably wanted to make a peaceful deal with France instead of going to war with them.

ANSWER SHEET

Week 4

⭐ Week 4 ⭐ Math

⭐ Topic 1 ⭐ Add & Subtract Negative Numbers

⭐ Page 51 ⭐

1. 6
2. -2
3. -5
4. 15
5. -12
6. 9

⭐ Topic 2 ⭐ Multiply & Divide Negative Numbers

⭐ Page 52 ⭐

1. 0
2. 54
3. Undefined
4. 4
5. 10
6. -2

⭐ Topic 3 ⭐ Convert Fractions to Decimals & Decimals to Fractions

⭐ Page 57 ⭐

1. 1.7
2. $7\frac{18}{25}$
3. 3.6
4. $10\frac{1}{50}$
5. $3.\overline{3}$
6. $3\frac{19}{20}$

⭐ Topic 4 ⭐ Real-World Problems Using Rational Numbers

⭐ Page 58 ⭐

1. 4 pounds
2. 12 miles
3. 2 times; $60
4. $12.25
5. $1.34
6. 4.3 feet below the surface of the water

⭐ Topic 5 ⭐ Ordering Rational Numbers

⭐ Page 61 ⭐

1. $\frac{7}{6}$, 1.2, $1\frac{9}{35}$
2. 4.05, $\frac{41}{10}$, $4\frac{1}{3}$
3. -2.9, $-\frac{11}{4}$, $-2\frac{3}{8}$
4. $-3\frac{1}{5}$, -3.1, -2.99
5. Circle $-1\frac{2}{5}$, $-1\frac{4}{9}$
6. Circle 0, -1.5, $-\frac{5}{2}$, $-\frac{8}{3}$

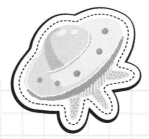

ANSWER SHEET

⭐ Week 4 ⭐ Language Review
⭐ Topic 1 ⭐ Verbal Shifts

⭐ Page 53 ⭐

1. Mario drank the milk so fast that he got stomach pains and nausea.
2. Angela completed her science homework; however, she did not get them all correct and received a failing grade.
3. When my mother and I arrived at the fancy restaurant, my dad had already eaten.
4. On the day of my soccer game, the sun was shining and the birds were singing.
5. My grandfather receives a hunting magazine every month but he barely ever reads it.
6. My little sister screamed when my mother put her on Santa's lap.

⭐ Week 4 ⭐ Writing
⭐ Topic 2 ⭐ Analyzing Both Sides Of An Issue

⭐ Page 54 ⭐

Answers will vary.
1. a. https://school-uniforms.procon.org/
   b. https://www.americanprep.org/what-are-good-reasons-for-wearing-school-uniforms/
   c. https://schoolsupplyboxes.com/blogs/school-blog/should-all-schools-require-students-to-wear-uniforms
2. a. School uniforms allow for equality.
   b. School uniforms reduce crime levels.
   c. School uniforms allow for people to focus on learning in the classroom.
3. a. https://school-uniforms.procon.org/
   b. https://www.newyorker.com/culture/culture-desk/the-unquestioned-goodness-of-school-uniforms
   c. https://writetheworld.com/groups/1/shared/61109/version/117031
4. a. School uniforms do not allow people to be original.
   b. School uniforms do not allow people to wear religious clothing.
   c. School uniforms require students to spend a lot of money which is hard on some families.
5. I would choose to write about how students should wear uniforms. I have a lot of evidence on this side, as well as strong points.

ANSWER SHEET

★ Week 4 ★ Reading

★ Topic 3 ★ Finding the Central Idea in NonFiction

★ Page 60 ★

1. Scientist proved that bats are not legally blind.
2. a. The study included lighting bugs.
   b. Bats recognized the light from the lighting bugs and avoided them.
   c. Bats do not like the taste of lightening bugs.
3. To inform
4. Scientists wanted to prove whether or not bats were blind like the age old saying. Through previous research, scientists from Purdue University realized that bats do not like lightening bugs. To prove whether or not they can see, scientists blacked out the light from lightning bugs to see if they would eat them, then they used regular lightning bugs. They noticed the light from the lightning bugs and avoided them, thus proving that they can see the light and that they are not blind.

★ Week 4 ★ Science

★ Topic 1 ★ Chemical Structure

★ Page 55-56 ★

1. A substance that undergoes a change
2. The result of an action
3. The temperature at which something melts and changes form
4. The degree of consistency
5. The ability to be dissolved
6. Answers may vary
7. When the coconut oil reached its melting point, it was more soluble with the other substances. The density of the soap fit the containers of the molds.

★ Week 4 ★ Social Studies

★ Topic 1 ★ The U.S. - Mexican War

★ Page 62 ★

1. A belief that settlers should spread out in North America
2. More land was discovered, an increase in trade
3. Slavery, war
4. Added
5. Answers may vary.

ANSWER SHEET

Week 5

★ Week 5 ★ Math

★ Topic 1 ★ Add & Subtract Linear Expressions

★ Page 64 ★

1. $x - 10$
2. $3x^2 + 3x + 9$
3. $-7x - 3$
4. $4a - 4b$
5. $-2j^2 - j - 1$
6. $5m^2 + m + 6$

★ Topic 2 ★ Expand Linear Expressions

★ Page 65 ★

1. $27x^3 - 15x^2$
2. $-14u + 22$
3. $x^3 + 8x^2 + 6x - 7$
4. $-a^3 + 4a^2 - 9a$
5. $-8xy^2 + 8xy - 8x$
6. $63a^2 + 5a - 2$

★ Topic 3 ★ Equivalent Expressions

★ Page 70 ★

1. No
2. Yes
3. No
4. Yes
5. No
6. No

★ Topic 4 ★ Powers Rational Numbers

★ Page 71 ★

1. x^{21}
2. 10^{28}
3. $x = 20$
4. g^2
5. h
6. b^4

★ Topic 5 ★ One-Step Inequalities

★ Page 74 ★

1. $x < \dfrac{5}{4}$
2. $y > -4$
3. $x \geq -3$
4. $c \geq 20$
5. $d > 8$
6. $f < 3$

ANSWER SHEET

★Week 5 ★ Reading
★ Topic 1 ★ Archetypes in Fiction

★ Page 67 ★

1. The hero character is Cinduri. She went from having nothing to marrying the Prince.
2. The archetypal mentor is the godfather. Since Cinduri's mother and father died, the godfather gave Cinduri advice.
3. The setting went from a poor location to a wealthy location.
4. The archetypal conflict is making the hero do chores, refusing to let her attend a party, and then attends from the presence of magic.
5. The archetypal villain is the stepmother, the one that caused the hero problems.

★Week 5 ★ Language
★ Topic 2 ★ Using Punctuation To Indicate Pauses

★ Page 72 ★

1. The ellipsis is used in order to take out information. The information that the writer took out was information they thought they didn't need.
2. This ellipsis shows that Mia was pausing and trying to think when speaking.
3. The dash was used to show an interruption. This was there because the story was interrupted by a car accident.

★ Week 5 ★ Writing
★ Topic 3 ★ Outlining An Argument

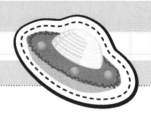

★ Page 73 ★

Answers will vary.
1. Students should be required to wear school uniforms.
    a. School uniforms diminish violence.
        I. Less thefts will occur inside the school.
        II. Outside people will not be able to sneak in.
        III. Teachers will be able to keep track of their own students.
    b. School uniforms eliminate distractions.
        I. Students will be able to focus on learning.
        II. Students will not be distracted by inappropriate clothing.
        III. Uniforms will eliminate jealousy amongst students.
    c. School uniforms help families save money.
        I. Named brand clothing is expensive.
        II. Parents will buy less clothing.
        III. School uniforms cost less.

ANSWER SHEET

★Week 5 ★ Science

★ Topic 1 ★ Velocity, Distance, and Time

★ Page 68-69 ★

1. The speed of something
2. The amount of space between two things
3. The measurement of seconds, minutes, etc.
4. 2.4 inches per minute
5. 120 meters per minute
6. 33.3 yards per second
7. Answers may vary.

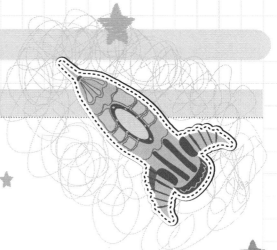

★Week 5 ★ Social Studies

★ Topic 1 ★ Northern and Central America

★ Page 75 ★

Answer may vary.

Week 6

★Week 6 ★ Math

★ Topic 1 ★ Two-Step Equations

★ Page 77 ★

1. $m = \dfrac{13}{3}$
2. $h = \dfrac{23}{12}$
3. $y = -20$
4. $x = \dfrac{4}{5}$
5. $j = -2$
6. $a = -2$

ANSWER SHEET

★ Topic 2 ★ Two-Step Equation Word Problems

★ Page 78 ★

1. $29 = 5 + 3m$; 8 miles
2. $6(p + 0.21) = 17.52$
3. $52 = 2w + 30$; $w = 11$ cm
4. $6(c - 8) = 204$ or $6c - 48 = 204$; 42 chickens
5. $2(2w) + 2w = 105$ or $6w = 105$; $w = 17.5$ ft and $l = 35$ ft
6. $1,950 = 600 + 6p$; $225

★ Topic 3 ★ Two-Step Equations with Decimals and Fractions

★ Page 83 ★

1. $y = -3$
2. $x = -\dfrac{35}{6}$
3. $a = 10$
4. $p = 18$
5. $j = -2.5$
6. $u = -\dfrac{8}{17}$

★ Topic 4 ★ Two-Step Inequalities

★ Page 84 ★

1. $y < 2$
2. $x \leq -3$
3. $b < \dfrac{1}{4}$
4. $t \leq 8$
5. $j < -8$
6. $k < -\dfrac{7}{3}$

★ Topic 5 ★ Two-Step Inequality Word Problems

★ Page 87 ★

1. $i \geq 105 + 128n$; $i \geq \$3,945$
2. $14 + 2s \leq 20$; $s \leq 3$
3. $12t - 500 \geq 800$; $t \geq 108.\overline{3}$ but since you can't sell $0.\overline{3}$ tickets, $t \geq 109$ in this situation
4. $5,000 \geq 3,000 + 125w$; $w \leq 16$ ® At most 16 weeks
5. $\dfrac{2}{3}n + 5 > 12$; $n > 10.5$
6. $50c - 15 \geq 25$; $c \geq 0.8$ ® You need to sell the cookies for at least $0.80 each

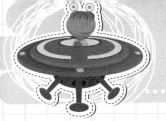

ANSWER SHEET

★ Week 6 ★ Writing
★ Topic 1 ★ Sources

★ Page 79 ★

Answers will vary.
1. Tokyo
2. a. https://www.britannica.com/place/Tokyo
   b. https://www.japan-guide.com/e/e2164.html
   c. https://www.history.com/news/six-things-you-should-know-about-tokyo
3. a. In the article "6 Things You Should Know About Tokyo" Barbara Maranzani explains that "a massive earthquake destroyed nearly half of Tokyo in 1923" (Maranzani).
   b. According to the Tokyo Guide, "a top attraction is the Imperial Palace" (Tokyo Guide).
   c. The Encyclopedia Britannica explains that "Tokyo had high rail system used for transportation" (Encyclopedia Britannica).

★ Week 6 ★ Writing
★ Topic 2 ★ Informative Essay

★ Page 80 ★

Answers will vary.
1. Ebola
2. a. https://www.webmd.com/a-to-z-guides/ebola-fever-virus-infection
   b. https://www.cdc.gov/vhf/ebola/about.html
   c. https://www.who.int/news-room/fact-sheets/detail/ebola-virus-disease
3. a. How do people get Ebola?
      I. Spreads through skin to skin contact
      II. Spreads through fluids of an infected animal
      III. Spreads through contaminated needles
   b. Symptoms of Ebola
      I. Flu like symptoms
      II. Bleeding of eyes, ears, and nose
      III. Rash
   c. How is Ebola treated?
      I. Blood transfusions
      II. Fluids and electrolytes
      III. Oxygen

ANSWER SHEET

★Week 6 ★ Reading
★ Topic 3 ★ Comparing Points of View

★ Page 86 ★
1. Third person point of view
2. She and her
3. First person point of view
4. Me, I, my
5. Both passages explain what happened to Malala.
6. The first passage is more informational while passage two is more personal.
7. Answers will vary

★Week 6 ★ Science
★ Topic 1 ★ Functions of the Plant Cell

★ Page 81 ★
1. A
2. H
3. I
4. D
5. G
6. F
7. K
8. E
9. B
10. J
11. C

★ Page 82 ★
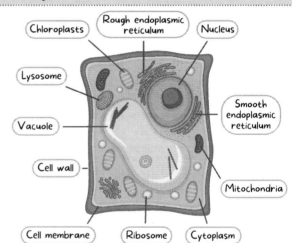

★Week 6 ★ Social Studies
★ Topic 1 ★ Purposes of Government

★ Page 88 ★
1. This is to keep people safe and to make sure people are following rules and laws.
2. Setting laws and making people adhere to them
3. Chaos would ensue and many people would get hurt.
4. People are in positions in order to keep citizens safe.
5. Police officers and the military
6. There would be a lot of fighting and a lot of crime.
7. To help people that need help
8. Social security
9. Many people would not have the services and care that they need.

ANSWER SHEET

Week 7

★ Week 7 ★ Math

★ Topic 1 ★ Scale Drawings

★ Page 90 ★

1. 2.25 in
2. 18 ft
3. About 2500 miles
4. 10.25"
5. 21 cm
6. 12.5 miles

★ Topic 2 ★ Construct Scale Drawings

★ Page 91 ★

1.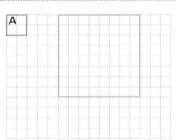

2.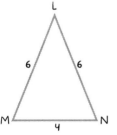

3.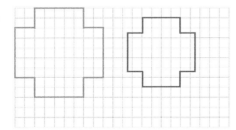

4.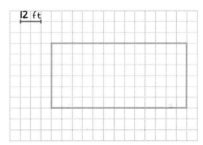

5.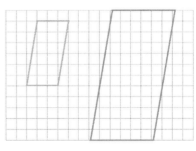

ANSWER SHEET

★ Topic 3 ★ Identify Scale Factor

★ Page 96 ★

1. 4
2. $\frac{3}{5}$
3. 22
4. 0.5
5. $\frac{5}{6}$
6. 4

★ Topic 4 ★ Triangle Side Lengths and Pythagorean Theorem

★ Page 97 ★

1. No, 2 + 3 ≯ 7
2. Yes
3. 1 + 2 ≯ 3
4. $\sqrt{21} \approx 4.58$
5. $\sqrt{10} \approx 3.16$
6. $\sqrt{580} \approx 24.083$ ft

★ Topic 5 ★ Plane Sections of 3D Figures

★ Page 100 ★

1. Circle
2. Triangle
3. Rectangle
4. Square
5. Triangle
6. Rectangle

★ Week 7 ★ Language

★ Topic 1 ★ Context Clues

★ Page 92-93 ★

1. Comfort and escape
   Desiree finds comfort in reading.
2. Disgust or hatred
   Since uncle Ernie works all the dime he hates when people are lazy.
3. To criticize or disapprove of
   The judge was criticizing the actions of the defendant in the courtroom.
4. Thinking something is true
   Using outside evidence of car tracks and the mail, the thieves thought that the Smiths were not home.

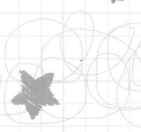
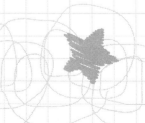

ANSWER SHEET

★ Week 7 ★ Reading
★ Topic 2 ★ Using Textual Evidence in Fiction

★ Page 98 ★

Answers may vary.

1. The stranger was nervous and was always looking around. The second adjective that describes the stranger is that he mysterious. The narrator mentions that "the stranger did not have the appearance of a man that rode the mast," however, he explained to the narrator that he grew up on the water. The third adjective that describes the stranger is that he was a loner. The narrator explains that he "was a very silent man by custom" and was always alone and quiet.

2. The narrator feels that he is lying. The stranger claims that he has been on the water his entire life; however, the narrator notes that "the stranger did not have the appearance of a man that rode the mast". The narrator and his father, the inn owner, feel that the strangers is hiding secrets.

3. The stranger has to be very important to the plot of the story. In the beginning of the passage, the narrator mentions that he was asked to write down "the entire particulars about the illustrious Treasure Island adventure". The stranger must be part of the narrator's adventure.

★ Week 7 ★ Writing
★ Topic 3 ★ Signal Shifts

★ Page 99 ★

1. A little girl named Suzie hit another little girl named Amaya while at recess. Suzie did not like that Amaya would not get off the swings, so she hit her. Immediately, the recess monitor noticed the situation. She told Suzie to come with her. At the end of recess, when Suzie's teacher went to pick up her class at the door, the recess monitor told Suzie's teacher that Suzie hit another child at recess. Mrs. Gooden, Suzie's teacher, was not pleased with Suzie's behavior. She had a conversation with Suzie about her temper, but Suzie was not listening, which made Mrs. Gooden upset. When Mrs. Gooden arrives in her classroom with her class, she calls down to the office. She tells the principal what Suzie had done and the principal tells Mrs. Gooden to send Suzie down to his office. Suzie walks very slowly to the principal's office, as she is scared about what will happen. When Suzie arrives at the principal's office, Mr. Terry, the principal, talks with Suzie about her behavior. Mr. Terry gives Suzie an after school detention for hitting another girl. He explains to Suzie that she has to serve her detention the following day.

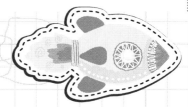

ANSWER SHEET

★ Page 99 ★

2. Erin has to get her wisdom teeth out on Tuesday at **8:00**am. When that day arrived, Erin arrived at her dentist office, Bright Smiles, bright and early at **7:30** in the morning. She checked in and was taken back to a room to lay back in a chair so the nursing assistant could numb the area they were working on. After that, Erin's dentist, Dr. Routch, gave her a shot so that she didn't feel anything when Dr. Routch removed Erin's four wisdom teeth. Time passed while the anesthesia was wearing off. At **9:15**, Erin woke up very groggy and she did not remember anything, which was normal. When released, Erin and her mother left and she took Erin home and put her to bed. Erin slept the entire day. She woke up at **6:30** in the evening and was in a lot of pain.

★Week7★ Science
★ Topic 1 ★ Functions of the Animal Cell

★ Page 94 ★

1. D
2. A
3. J
4. E
5. I
6. G
7. E
8. B
9. F
10. H

★ Page 95 ★

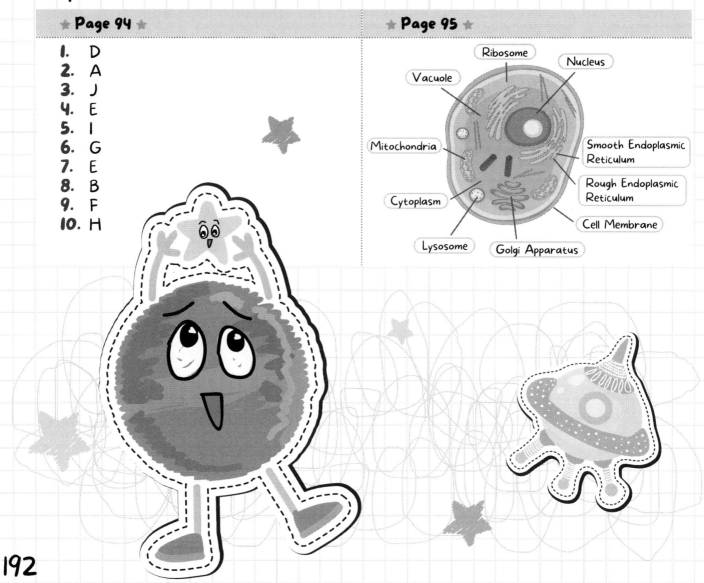

ANSWER SHEET

★Week 7 ★ Social Studies
★ Topic 1 ★ South America

★ Page 101 ★

1. a. North America
   b. South America
   c. Central America
   d. The Carribean
2. a. Asia
   b. Africa
   c. North America
3. Spanish
4. Table Top Mountains
5. The Equator
6. The Tropic of Capricorn
7. These answers may vary
   a. The highest point is Cerro Aconcagua which is in the Andes Mountains. This is in the country of Argentina.
   b. The largest country in South America is Brazil.
   c. The official language of Brazil is Portugese and not Spanish.
   d. The highest waterfall in the world is found in South America. It is called Angel Falls.
   e. The driest place on Earth is located in South America. It is the Atacama Desert in the country of Chile.

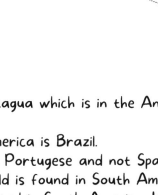

Week 8

★ Week 8 ★ Math

★ Topic 1 ★ Radius and Diameter

★ Page 103 ★

1. 5.5
2. 1
3. True
4. 4.5 cm
5. 12 meters
6. $\dfrac{x}{2}$

★ Topic 2 ★ Area of a Circle

★ Page 104 ★

1. 144π square feet
2. 81π square cm
3. $4y^2\pi$
4. 2 mm
5. $\dfrac{75}{4}\pi$
6. 8π

ANSWER SHEET

★ Topic 3 ★ Circumference of a Circle

★ Page 109 ★

1. 10π ft
2. 12π in
3. 40.5 mm
4. 1.5 m
5. 0.75π in
6. 6π ft

★ Topic 4 ★ Complementary, Supplementary & Vertical Angles

★ Page 110 ★

1. 18°
2. 108°
3. $(90 - b)°$
4. $(180 - b)°$
5. 45.5°
6. 20°

★ Topic 5 ★ Transformations

★ Page 113 ★

1.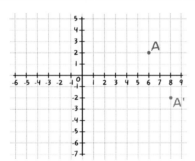

2.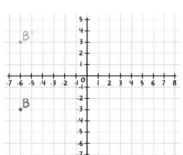

3.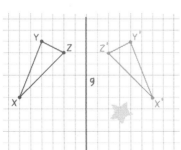

4. a, c, d
5. 5 units
6.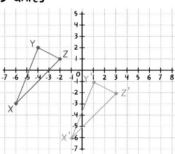

ANSWER SHEET

★ Week 8 ★ Language
★ Topic 1 ★ Advanced Root Words

★ Page 105 ★

1. Incredible, incredulous, credible
   Joyce was a credible witness for the defense team in the trial.
2. Rebellion, embellish, belligerent
   During the U.S-Mexican war, the Mexicans started a rebellion against the United States.
3. Democracy, democratic, bureaucracy
   Pete Buttigieg is running for president in the democratic party.
4. Hemoglobin, hemophilia, hemorrhage
   My cousin Violet has hemophilia, which is a disease that causes her blood to clot improperly.
5. Marine, maritime, marsh
   The aquatic plants we have been collecting grow profusely in the marsh.
6. Dispel, expel, propel
   The machine expels fluid when you push the level down.

★ Week 8 ★ Writing
★ Topic 2 ★ Transitions

★ Page 106 ★

Answer may vary (1 - 6 questions).
1. My father used his outdoor fryer to cook the Thanksgiving turkey; however, he left the turkey in there for over an hour which burnt the turkey.
2. Our family arrived at the airport two hours early for our flight to the Bahamas, but we had to wait six more hours due to a delay.
3. The store owner counted the money in the register at the end of the day and realized that three hundred dollars was missing. Therefore, the store owner called the police and an investigation began.
4. My husband was the winner of the trivia contest at work and won home tickets to the Lakers, therefore we are planning to go next week.
5. Because my left back tire was flat, I had to call a tow truck.
6. therefore
7. Even though
8. Meanwhile
9. however
10. first

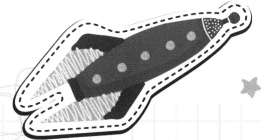

ANSWER SHEET

★ Week 8 ★ Reading
★ Topic 3 ★ Nonfiction Paragraph Structure

★ Page 112 ★

1. Astronomers and scientists have found that a planet just outside of our solar system can potentially hold life.
2. This newly discovered planet is called K2-18b and has temperatures that are ideal for humans and are similar to the temperatures on Earth. K2-18b is not extremely hot or cold like other planets in our solar system.
3. Water vapor has also been found on this new planet, which is located just outside the Leo star system.
4. To explain that scientists discovered a new planet
5. To explain the qualities of the new planet
6. To explain the differences between the new planet and Earth

★ Week 8 ★ Science
★ Topic 1 ★ The Rock Cycle

★ Page 108 ★

1. A rock
2.
   * formed through the cooling of magma and lava
     * crystallization.
   * have undergone a transformation through heat and or pressure
     * metamorphism.
   * formed by the elements; rock or air
     * sedimentation.

★ Week 8 ★ Social Studies
★ Topic 1 ★ The French and Indian War

★ Page 114 ★

1. The British and the French were fighting over land in North America.
2. The British and the French were settling in America. Soon, the land began to become occupied and both countries were fighting over who owned what land. They wanted specific land like the Ohio River Valley due to the rich soil in the area. Because the British did not think the French had many citizens, they sent George Washington over to tell them to leave or they would fight. The French refused so George Washington and his men fought against France, but they surrendered because they were outnumbered. Each country sent over more and more troops and many Native Americans chose their side. They went to war, and many died, but ultimately the British won.

ANSWER SHEET

Week 9

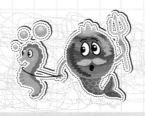

★ Week 9 ★ Math

★ Topic 1 ★ Making Inferences from Random Samples

★ Page 116 ★

1. 225 students
2. 875 people
3. 270 students
4. 400 employees
5. 12,500 cordless vacuums

★ Topic 2 ★ Making Inferences about Two Populations

★ Page 117 ★

1. Yes, first period had higher scores
2. b
3. b
4. false

★ Topic 3 ★ Probability Models

★ Page 122 ★

1. 0.1
2.

Color Car	Probability
Silver	$\frac{11}{30}$ or 0.37
White	$\frac{4}{15}$ or 0.27
Black	$\frac{1}{5}$ or 0.2
Red	$\frac{1}{15}$ or 0.07
Green	$\frac{1}{10}$ or 0.1

3. $\frac{5}{23}$
4. 0.65
5. 60%
6. $\frac{12}{25}$ or 0.48

ANSWER SHEET

★ Topic 4 ★ Approximating Probability of a Chance Event

★ Page 123 ★

1. $\frac{1}{2}$ or 0.5
2. $\frac{3}{10}$ or 0.3
3. $\frac{1}{2}$ or 0.5
4. $\frac{1}{4}$ or 0.25
5. $\frac{1}{5}$ or 0.2
6. $\frac{3}{20}$ or 0.15

★ Topic 5 ★ Experimental Probability

★ Page 126 ★

1. $\frac{3}{25}$ or 0.12
2. $\frac{3}{8}$ or 0.375
3. $\frac{1}{8}$ or 0.125
4. $\frac{12}{55}$ or 0.218
5. $\frac{1}{5}$ or 0.2
6. $\frac{4}{125}$ or 0.032

★ Week 9 ★ Reading

★ Topic 1 ★ Theme

★ Page 119 ★

1. A theme is a main idea or underlying message.
2. Themes of patience and understanding can be found in this story.
3. The character of Alice develops this theme because she really wants the Caterpillar to listen to her and answer her questions. The character of the Caterpillar does not listen to her at all. This causes Alice frustration, but the Caterpillar just wants her to be patient and listen to him instead.
4. The setting develops this theme because one side of the mushroom makes Alice grow taller and the other side shorter; however, Alice does not get her question answered and she doesn't know which side she should choose.
5. The Caterpillar annoying and frustrating Alice contributes to this theme because Alice needs her question answered in order to solve the mystery of her height.

ANSWER SHEET

★ Week 9 ★ Language
★ Topic 2 ★ Use Reference Materials

★ Page 124 ★

1. Having more than one meaning
2. Obscure, dubious, unclear
3. To become adjusted
4. Accommodate, adapt, conform
5. To reprimand or to criticize harshly
6. Complement, flatter, praise
7. To ban or stop from using
8. Accept, allow, welcome
9. Adjective
   We are going to have a pop quiz in English in the imminent future
10. Noun
    We are studying the theory of relativity in science

★ Week 9 ★ Writing
★ Topic 3 ★ Creating A Setting

★ Page 125 ★

Answers will vary.
1. There is a large circular table, one large window, thirteen orange chairs, an orange and white wall, and a black trash can.
2. When you first walk into the room, the bright orange colors of the side wall and the thirteen chairs grab your attention. The smooth large circular table is a great place to study and complete your work. Since the large window and the door is made of glass, you can hear the chaos in the halls very easily. I smell the remains of an old lunch tray in the black trash can.
3. Answer vary.

ANSWER SHEET

★ Week 9 ★ Science

★ Topic 1 ★ Structure and Function of Organic Compound Groups

★ Page 120 ★

1. A chemical compound that contains carbon.
2. Carbohydrates - provide and store energy; structural element
   a. Carbon, hydrogen, oxygen
   b. Simple sugars
3. Lipids - store energy
   a. Fats
4. Proteins - energy source, form tissues, help with chemical reactions
   a. Amino acids
5. Nucleic Acids - helps transfer genetic information
   a. DNA

★ Topic 2 ★ Ecosystems

★ Page 121 ★

Answers will vary.
* Cold Desert Ecosystems

   Organisms - **Jackrabbits**
   Location - **Greenland**
* Temperate Deciduous Forest Ecosystems

   Organisms - **White-tailed deer**
   Location - **Eastern United States**
* Taiga Ecosystems

   Organisms - **Bears**
   Location - **Canada**
* Prairie Grassland Ecosystems

   Organisms - **Eagles**
   Location - **North and South Dakota, Kansas**
* Savanna Grassland

   Organisms - **Elephants**
   Location - **Africa**
* Hot Desert Ecosystems

   Organisms - **RockHopper Penguin**
   Location - **Sahara desert**

ANSWER SHEET

★ Week 9 ★ Social Studies

★ Topic 1 ★ Primary and Secondary Sources

★ Page 127 ★

1. Type of Source - Secondary
   Explanation - It was given out in 1960 during the election.
2. Type of Source - Secondary
   Explanation - It was not written during the Renaissance time period.
3. Type of Source - Primary
   Explanation - It was written in 1901 during the war.
4. Type of Source - Secondary
   Explanation - It was not written during that time period.
5. Type of Source - Secondary
   Explanation - It was not written by Oprah during that particular time.
6. Type of Source - Primary
   Explanation - It was written during that particular time period.

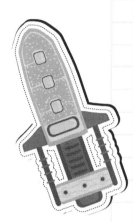

Week 10

★ Week 10 ★ Math

★ Topic 1 ★ Making Inferences from Random Samples

★ Page 129 ★

1. Event A
2. They have the same probabilities: 0.5
3. Red
4. 7:55
5. His experimental probability was 0.45 which is 0.05 less than the theoretical probability of 0.5.
6. Florida

ANSWER SHEET

★ Topic 2 ★ Scatter Plots

★ Page 130 ★

1. a
2. d
3. b
4. a

★ Topic 3 ★ The Counting Principle

★ Page 135 ★

1. 24
2. 2,250
3. 72
4. 45
5. 62,320,000
6. 260

★ Topic 4 ★ Sample Space of Compound Events

★ Page 136 ★

1. 1H, 1T, 2H, 2T, 3H, 3T, 4H, 4T, 5H, 5T, 6H, 6T

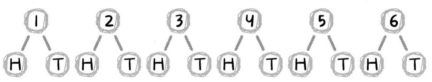

2. 36
3. 36
4. 80
5.

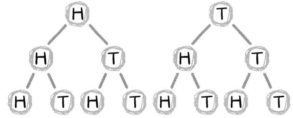

6. 15

★ Topic 5 ★ Probabilities of Compound Events

★ Page 139 ★

1. $\dfrac{1}{12}$
2. $\dfrac{1}{2}$
3. $\dfrac{1}{4}$
4. $\dfrac{1}{8}$
5. $\dfrac{1}{4}$
6. $\dfrac{1}{36}$

ANSWER SHEET

★ Week 10 ★ Language
★ Topic 1 ★ Verbal Irony and Puns

★ Page 131 ★

1. clear as mud for me
   This is an example of verbal irony because it shows that the student did not understand the lesson at all.
2. fun as plucking my eyebrows
   This is an example of verbal irony because the grandson did not have fun painting the basement or removing the carpet.
3. exciting as going to the dentist and getting my teeth pulled
   This is an example of verbal irony because the student thought the science experiments were not exciting at all.
4. glue salesman; stuck
   The pun is glue salesman and the word stuck.
5. shocked; struck by lighting
   The pun is struck by lighting and the word shocked.
6. Santa; nick of time
   The pun is Santa and the phrase "the nick of time", referring to Santa's first name Nick or Nicholas.

★ Week 10 ★ Writing
★ Topic 2 ★ Narrative Conclusions

★ Page 132 ★

Answers may vary.

★ Week 10 ★ Reading
★ Topic 3 ★ Narrative Conclusions

★ Page 138 ★

1. The purpose is to inform and to persuade.
2. The author's viewpoint is that people should recycle.
3. Yes, the author appeals to pathos. He or she explains how big the patch is and that this issue is caused because people are not recycling.
4. Yes, the author appeals to the audience's logos. The author uses logic by explaining what the garbage patch looks like and how it got there.
5. The author's tone is objective and passionate.

ANSWER SHEET

★ Week 10 ★ Science
★ Topic 1 ★ Genotypes and Phenotypes

★ Page 133-134 ★

1. A unit of heredity that is passed down from parents
2. Alternate forms of genes
3. The genetic construction of an organism
4. Set of observable characteristics
5. Baby number six is blue.
6. The puppy is dark brown.
7. Leo is gray, Elray is white, and Gina is a mixture of gray and white.

★ Week 10 ★ Social Studies
★ Topic 1 ★ The Middle East

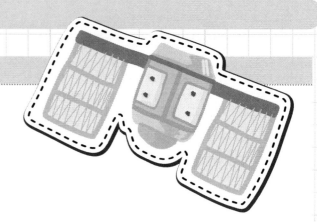

★ Page 140 ★

1. a. Asia
   b. Africa
2. a. Mediterranean Sea
   b. Black Sea
   c. Caspian Sea
   d. Red Sea
   e. Persian Gulf
   f. Arabian Sea
3. a. Nile River
   b. Jordan River
   c. Tigris-Euphrates River
4. a. Oil
   b. Natural gas
5. a. The most common languages spoken in The Middle East are Arabic, Persian, and Turkish.
   b. The Dead Sea is at 420 meters below sea level which makes it the lowest point on Earth.
   c. The tallest building in the world is located in the United Arab Emirates.
   d. Hamsters were discovered in Syria.
   e. Mocha was made in The Middle East before coming to America.

ANSWER SHEET

Week 11

★ Week 11 ★ Math

★ Topic 1 ★ Review Week 1
★ Page 142 ★

1. $1\frac{4}{5}$ mile
2. 12
3. No
4. The price per video game
5. $49
6. $\frac{2}{5}$ or 0.4

★ Topic 2 ★ Review Week 2
★ Page 143 ★

1. 40
2. $d = 2c$
3. $y = \frac{1}{4}x$
4. B
5. $14.59
6. $w = \frac{100}{3}t$

★ Topic 3 ★ Review Week 3
★ Page 148 ★

1. Negative
2. 3
3. -2.5
4. $\frac{55}{12}$ or $4\frac{7}{12}$
5. $\frac{32}{13}$ or $2\frac{6}{13}$
6. $-\frac{8}{7}$ or $-1\frac{1}{7}$

★ Topic 4 ★ Review Week 4
★ Page 149 ★

1. $1\frac{13}{20}$
2. $1.2\overline{6}$
3. -23
4. 132
5. 9.02, 9.1, $9\frac{1}{8}$
6. $38.25

★ Topic 5 ★ Review Week 5
★ Page 152 ★

1. $5x^2 + x - 7$
2. $-11a^2 - 20a$
3. No
4. a^{10}
5. x^5
6. $a \geq 23$

ANSWER SHEET

★ Week 11 ★ Language
★ Topic 1 ★ Antonyms and Synonyms

★ Page 144 ★

1. Words that are similar to another
2. Words that are the opposite

1. lavish
2. skeptical
3. genius
4. accomplished
5. economical
6. Janice decorated her Christmas tree with economical ornaments she gathered from the thrift store.
7. confident
8. Mr. Gen was confident that Taryn and Leo cheated on the math final as he had a lot of proof that it happened.
9. imbecile
10. Eric is a musical imbecile. He is forty seven years old and went to college for music, but he can't carry a tune.
11. unskilled
12. William is an unskilled woodworker. He has not crafted anything more than a crooked wooden box.

★ Week 11 ★ Reading
★ Topic 2 ★ Dialogue

★ Page 145 ★

1. The dialogue reveals that he does not want to attend college after high school graduation.
2. The dialogue reveals that Jake's father disagrees with Jake's decision to not attend college. He explains that he regrets not going to college.
3. Yes, this is the best way for the audience to understand the characters. This also helps create conflict.

★ Week 11 ★ Reading
★ Topic 3 ★ Evaluating An Argument

★ Page 151 ★

Some answers may vary.
1. The author has three reasons why animals should be used in medical testing.
2. The first reason is that animal testing has helped many individuals. I agree with this because without these animals, many people would die without medicines or vaccines.
3. Taking a life for a life is not ethical.

ANSWER SHEET

4. Animals and humans have similar body types and body systems. I agree that they do have similar body types and systems; however, I do not think this is necessarily a strong reason why humans should die for this.
5. Humans can be used just as easily as animals.
6. Testing on animals eliminates death of humans. I agree with this because human lives are important.
7. Human lives should be equal to animal lives.

★Week 11 ★ Science
★ Topic 1 ★ Punnett Squares
★ Page 147 ★

1.

BB	Bb
Bb	bb

2.

GG	Gg
Gg	gg

★Week 11 ★ Social Studies
★ Topic 1 ★ The Beginning of the Civil War
★ Page 153 ★

During the time of the Civil War, the South wanted to be separated from the United States. Their plan was to have a country called the Confederate States of America. However, after four years of fighting in a cruel and bloody war, it finally ended and the South lost the war. This meant that slavery ended. However, just because they were free at the end of the war didn't mean too much since the former slaves did not have money or means of finding a job.

The time after the war ended was called the Reconstruction Era. The Republicans at that time wanted to reconstruct or change the South. They wanted to replace the current leaders, construct more schools so African Americans could learn, build and construct railroads for trade, and lower taxes on businesses. To go against these changes, many Caucasian Democrats created violent groups like the Ku Klux Klan and there was a lot of hatred towards the African Americans.

In 1866, an important change occurred in the Reconstruction Era. A law passed in Congress which gave that African Americans rights to write up contracts. This allowed African Americans to get control over what was theirs. This allowed African Americans to buy and own items, to work, own land, and to get married.

ANSWER SHEET

Week 12

Week 12 ★ Math

★ Topic 1 ★ Review Week 6

★ Page 155 ★

1. $k = -\frac{20}{3}$
2. $f = 13$
3. $2w + 2(3w) = 72$ or $8w = 72$; dimensions: 9ft x 27ft
4. $y = -2.4$
5. $a < \frac{1}{2}$
6. $8w - 60 \geq 500$; $w \geq 70$, they need to sell at least 70 car washes

★ Topic 2 ★ Review Week 7

★ Page 156 ★

1. 1.75 inches
2.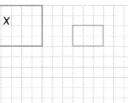
3. $\frac{1}{6}$
4. No, $1 + 1 \not> 2$
5. $\sqrt{40} \approx 6.32$
6. square

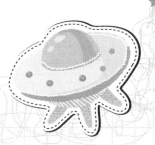

★ Topic 3 ★ Review Week 8

★ Page 161 ★

1. $36°$
2. $101°$
3. 81π square meters
4. 30π centimeters
5. $(-4,4)$
6. c

★ Topic 4 ★ Review Week 9

★ Page 162 ★

1. $\frac{1}{4}$ or 0.25
2. $\frac{1}{2}$ or 0.5
3. $\frac{1}{5}$ or 0.2
4. 25,000
5. b
6. $\frac{5}{19}$

ANSWER SHEET

★ Topic 5 ★ Review Week 10

★ Page 165 ★

1. a
2. false
3. $\dfrac{10}{47}$
4. 168
5. $\dfrac{1}{36}$
6. $\dfrac{1}{16}$

★ Week 12 ★ Language

★ Topic 1 ★

★ Page 157 ★

1. Words based on feeling and emotion
2. Words based on the dictionary definition of a word
3. denotation
4. connotation
5. denotation
6. denotation
7. denotation
8. connotation

★ Week 12 ★ Writing

★ Topic 2 ★ Editing Practice

★ Page 158 ★

   Adults and teenagers alike have their cellphones close at hand, and frequently look at them whenever they can. Individuals take their cellphones with them wherever they go, but should students bring their cellphones to school with them?

   It is a fact that many students own cell phones and those numbers continue to climb in recent years. Students are getting their first cell phones at a young age. Children as young as fourth or fifth grade can be seen with a cell phone in their hands, and they bring their cellphones to school.

   There has been a lot of controversy surrounding whether or not cell phones should be allowed in schools, and the consensus has yet to be decided regarding this issue. Depending on individual school systems, they will decide if students can bring phones to school.

209

ANSWER SHEET

Many school officials do not want cell phones brought into schools because they feel it will be a major distraction. They feel that students will be more focused on social media and texting their friends, than focused on the subjects they are learning. Many high schools and middle schools have made a rule that cell phones are to be put away in their students' pockets or bookbags during class. Other the other hand, teachers embrace this type of technology and incorporate the use of cellphones into what they are learning in class.

Other rules that have been implemented regarding cell phone use include students using their phones only during recess, passing periods, and lunch. However, many disagree with students using their phones during lunch because they feel that this diminishes interaction with other students. They fear that students will lose face to face conversations if they have their phones to focus on during this time.

With fear that cell phones will become a distraction, why do parents want their child to bring a cell phone to school? The major reason is safety. Parents want their children to have a phone in case of an emergency.

★ Week 12 ★ Reading

★ Topic 3 ★ Conflicting Information

★ Page 164 ★

1. a. Using animals as testing subjects is inaccurate
   b. Using animals as testing subjects is accurate
2. Answers will vary. I can see both sides of this and it will not be accurate all of the time, but animal testing has led to findings of medicines and cures and has saved lives. I agree with passage two.
3. a. Animals are not treated with care.
   b. Animals are treated with care.
4. Answers will vary. The first passage was more persuasive because it talked about how scientists burned and broken the bones of the animals.

★ Week 12 ★ Science

★ Topic 1 ★ Cellular Respiration

★ Page 160 ★

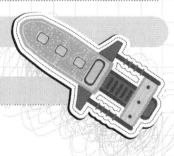

1. Glucose
2. Sugar
3. Glucose and Oxygen
4. Carbon Dioxide and Water
5. In cellular respiration, the cells use the food in your body to produce energy. In the reaction, the cells use glucose from the food we eat and oxygen to turn that into energy. What is left over is water and carbon dioxide.

ANSWER SHEET

★Week 12 ★ Social Studies
★ Topic 1 ★ The Beginning of the Civil War

★ Page 166 ★

1. A war between groups in the same country.
2. This is hard because it breaks up the country.
3. a. North
   b. South
4. Abraham Lincoln
5. Slavery
6. The Confederacy
7. The American Civil War started because the south did not agree with the north and the President of the United States.

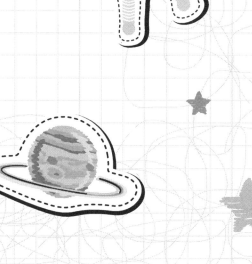

Printed in Poland
by Amazon Fulfillment
Poland Sp. z o.o., Wrocław